The Leadership Detour:
How the Unexpected Path Shaped My Success

The Leadership Detour:
How the Unexpected Path Shaped My Success

BY
Dr. Tammi Fleming

With formatting support by Euferose Correa White

Copyright © 2025 by Dr. Tammi Fleming

All rights reserved. No part of this publication may be reproduced, stored in a retrieval system, or transmitted in any form or by any means—electronic, mechanical, photocopy, recording, or otherwise—without prior written permission of the author, except by a reviewer who may quote brief passages in a review.

ISBN: 979-8-9986680-0-5 (hardcover)

Library of Congress Control Number: 2025908491

This is a work of nonfiction. Some names and identifying details have been changed to protect the privacy of individuals.

Subjects: Leadership—Personal Growth; Executive Coaching; Self-Reflection; Women in Leadership; Career Development

Classification: BUSINESS & ECONOMICS / Leadership; SELF-HELP / Personal Growth / Success

Publication Date: September 18, 2025

Cover design by David Colón, Colonfilm

Interior formatting and editorial support by Euferose Correa White

Illustrations by Destiny White

Published in the United States by

Diamond Consultants, LLC

[diamondconsultantsllc.com]

[info@diamondconsultantsllc.com]

Printed in the United States of America.

Dedication

Barbara Ann Jackson & Josephine Fleming

Two women, two paths, one deep well of love.

To Barbara, my guardian, my guiding light and the fiercest leader I've ever known. This book is a tribute to your legacy, your love, and your relentless pursuit of justice.

To Josephine, my birth mother, whose love I never doubted. Though your demons kept you from raising us, your pride in me never wavered. This book also belongs to you—for the strength it took to let go.

In memory and in honor.

Epigraph

The Leadership Detour

Because becoming who you are meant to be

is rarely a straight line.

Table of Contents

Introduction: The Leadership Detour................................. *xiii*

I: FOUNDATIONS OF LEADERSHIP

Chapter 1: *Where I Started*.. 1
Chapter 2: *Lessons in Belonging*... 31
Chapter 3: *The First Detour—The Gap Between Talent and Leadership*.. 58

II. NAVIGATING THE DETOURS

Chapter 4: *Hitting a Wall—When Hard Work Isn't Enough*........... 88
Chapter 5: *The Breakthrough*... 116
Chapter 6: *Mastering Emotional Intelligence*......................... 139

III: STEPPING INTO LEADERSHIP WITH INTENTION

Chapter 7: *Owning Your Voice & Executive Presence*............... 172
Chapter 8: *Building a Leadership Mindset for the Long Game*...... 199
Chapter 9: *Leadership as Legacy: Becoming the Leader You Needed*... 228
Acknowledgments.. 251
Glossary of Key Terms... 255
Resources & References.. 257
About the Author.. 259
A Note on the Interior Design and Visual Storytelling............ 260

Foreword

This book arrives at a critical moment. Many of us are struggling to get on the road toward thriving. Structural obstacles and emotional detours have stalled our journeys. None of us is immune, and too many of us are navigating these challenges in silence.

In *The Leadership Detour*, Dr. Tammi Fleming offers a way forward. With clarity and compassion, she helps readers recognize what stands in their way and equips them with the tools to move ahead with greater ease, deeper confidence, and renewed joy.

Tammi and I met during a detour in my professional journey. I was leading the GrassROOTS Community Foundation (GCF), an organization I co-founded to empower girls to become leaders and changemakers in their communities. I believed strongly in the work, but at that moment, it and I felt underappreciated and undervalued. Tammi held a leadership position at a national foundation, and officially, she was my program officer. But in reality, she was much more.

She saw value in what others overlooked. She championed me when my confidence wavered, and my work felt invisible. She offered thoughtful critique, tangible resources, and —most importantly— a belief in my potential that helped me reclaim my voice and vision. With her support, I got back on track and soared to new heights.

From the beginning, I trusted her brilliance and her ability to offer critique rooted in evidence and care. Her unassuming style made her easy to learn from. Over time, our professional relationship evolved into a genuine partnership—grounded in justice, shaped by challenge, and strengthened by mutual respect.

A moment I will never forget: Tammi once told me she had chosen to take speech lessons—not to change her voice, but to find it. That decision speaks volumes about who she is. She understood that how we speak—and how others hear us—are both personal and political. To lead, we sometimes must learn new languages. Tammi helps others do the same—and more.

This philosophy is embedded in my leadership and writing, particularly in my book, *Parent Like It Matters: How to Raise Joyful Changemaking Girls,* where I explore the concept of *mother leadership*. At its core, mother leadership means attending to who you are, recognizing your strengths, and knowing when you are off track. It means investing in yourself and building a community to get back on the path. And above all, it centers joy as both a compass and a source of power.

In training girls to lead, I emphasize the importance of recognizing detours and pivoting intentionally. Tammi exemplifies this. She has supported many facing career challenges, doubting their roles, or questioning the significance of their leadership. She has coached hundreds of senior leaders across various sectors, facilitated leadership retreats, and helped shape national strategies to promote equity, impact, and executive presence. Her influence and impact are undeniable.

In *The Leadership Detour*, readers can learn from Tammi as I—and many others—have. Page after page, she shares her keen insights, life experiences, and hard-earned wisdom. This isn't just a book of tools—it's a journey of reflection and growth. If you've ever hit a wall in your career, questioned your role, or wondered if your leadership matters, this book will meet you exactly where you are. Tammi will guide you with honesty, grace, and the kind of wisdom that is earned through experience.

—Janice Johnson Dias, PhD

Preface

Dear Reader,

Before we begin, let me tell you who I am today.

I am Dr. Tammi Fleming—mother, change-maker, strategist, and executive coach. I've spent decades in leadership roles across philanthropy, government, and nonprofits. I've coached many leaders, shaped national strategies, and built a life that once felt out of reach.

But I didn't arrive here on a straight path.

I wrote *The Leadership Detour* because my story—and maybe yours too—was never linear. It was full of sharp turns, invisible ceilings, and quiet reckonings that never made it onto my résumé. I wrote this book because I needed to tell the truth—not just about what I've done, but about what I've learned.

For years, the idea of writing a book lingered quietly in the background of my life—a whisper I promised to answer when things slowed down, when I felt more accomplished, or when I finally believed I had something "book-worthy" to say. But life rarely slows down, and readiness is often just another name for fear.

The truth is, my leadership detour started long before I stepped in a professional space. I was born in the housing projects of New Orleans, into a world shaped by poverty, instability, and silence. I started school late—my mother hadn't registered me until child welfare got involved. My siblings and I experienced the foster care system. I became a mother at 19. I learned to survive before I ever learned to lead.

And still—I rose.

Somewhere along the way, I became "successful." I earned degrees, gained recognition, and eventually landed what felt like my dream job. Even then, something felt off. I was working hard, doing all the right things—but I didn't understand why things weren't clicking. Why I wasn't advancing the way I expected. Why I felt stuck in rooms I'd worked so hard to enter. I lacked the self-awareness to realize that others were receiving my energy differently than I intended. I couldn't see the disconnect between how I saw myself and how I was showing up.

Those moments—the tension between my effort and my outcomes—left me searching for answers I couldn't always find in real time. So, I started writing. Not with the goal of becoming an author, but as a way to survive my own questions. I didn't keep a formal journal, but I always kept notes—pages and pages of thoughts, reflections, and workplace moments I needed to process. Writing helped me make sense of things I couldn't always say aloud.

Then last year, as I was wrapping up my time at the Department of Labor, a couple of conversations nudged me—hard—toward the truth I'd been circling: it was time to write the book. Not someday. Now.

In August, I sat down and began outlining what this book could become. I didn't know where it would take me, but I knew I had to follow the thread.

Along the way, I found myself reflecting not just on what I'd experienced—but on how I'd come to understand those experiences. One of the biggest shifts in my growth came when I was introduced to coaching—not as a profession, but as a practice. I had never even considered having a coach. But having someone hold space for me, ask the right questions, and create room for me to process and pivot—that was transformative. It changed how I lead. It changed how I live. Coaching helped me find language for things I had long buried. It helped me come home to myself.

And at the center of it all is Barbara Jackson—my guardian, my grounding, and the fiercest leader I've ever known. Barbara didn't just raise me—she formed me. This book begins with her brilliance because it is a part of her legacy. I am a part of her legacy. She taught me what it means to lead with integrity, to protect what matters, and to speak truth even when it's costly. And—strangely enough—we share the same birthday. I carry that fact like a secret flame. I hope this book honors her in a way that is fitting, fierce, and full of love.

Writing *The Leadership Detour* has been one of the most vulnerable, courageous, and clarifying things I've ever done. It forced me to revisit old wounds and name truths I once buried beneath performance. It asked me to speak not just from my résumé, but from my reckoning. This wasn't just writing. It was releasing. It was reclaiming.

This book is for the ones still on the journey. It's for the ones who know what it means to rise, fall, and rise again.

I wrote The Leadership Detour not as a manual, but as a mirror. A companion for every leader who has ever felt out of place on the path to purpose. It's part memoir, part message, and all truth.

If you've ever questioned whether you belong....
If you've ever found yourself detoured from the plan you made...

If you've ever been celebrated for your expertise but overlooked as a leader...

I hope this book helps you see that your detour didn't disqualify you—it prepared you.

There's still power in the pivot.

There's still purpose in the pause.

And there's still time to become the leader you were always meant to be.

With love,
Tammi Fleming

Introduction: The Leadership Detour

It doesn't make sense—I'm perfect for this role.

You've done everything they told you to do. You showed up early, stayed late, took feedback, kept your head down, worked twice as hard. You kept showing up, kept producing, kept proving yourself. Maybe you even got promoted. On paper, everything looks right.

So why does it still feel like you're stuck?

That question—what is happening?—is one too many of us have carried silently. Especially if you're a Black woman navigating professional spaces where your brilliance is celebrated but your leadership is questioned. Especially if you've found yourself hitting invisible walls after doing all the visible work.

This book was written for you.

For the woman who's accomplished but exhausted.

For the one who's ready but overlooked.

For the leader in the middle of a pivot she didn't see coming.

For the one asking, *What am I missing? And what do I do next?*

Leadership, for many of us, has never been just about skill—it's been about survival, translation, and recalibration. Especially for Black women and other marginalized leaders, the detour isn't rare—its routine. We ascend without blueprints. We lead while healing. We lead while questioning.

And still—we rise.

This book is my way of asking collective questions.

How do we rise with purpose when the path stops making sense?

How do we lead with truth in rooms that weren't built for our presence?

I call it *The Leadership Detour* because I believe every powerful leader reaches a point where the old rules stop working. Not because we failed—but because the road ahead requires a deeper kind of becoming.

The Leadership Detour isn't a step-by-step manual, it's a mirror, a companion, and a call. Through personal narrative, leadership insights, and coaching prompts, this book invites you to rethink what it means to lead—and what might be holding you back when technical excellence is no longer enough.

The "detour" I write about isn't failure. It's the moment

your internal growth needs to catch up to your external success. It's the turning point where the old tools stop working—not because you're not capable, but because your leadership is evolving.

Each chapter in this book blends:
- Storytelling rooted in lived experience
- Leadership reflections and hard-earned insights
- Coaching prompts to deepen your awareness and unlock next steps

At the end of every chapter, you'll find space to pause, reflect, and begin again. And for those who want to go deeper, there is a **Companion Guide** available—designed to help you unpack each theme with more structure, more intention, and more space to grow.

You can read this book straight through, or take it one chapter at a time. Some pages may feel like confirmation. Others may feel like confrontation. But all of it is designed to help you move from stuck to self-aware, from doubt to clarity, from exhaustion to alignment.

I've walked this detour myself—navigating success, invisibility, power, and purpose. This book is drawn from lived experience, shaped by years of coaching leaders through their own turning points.

You won't find quick fixes here.

What you will find is truth. Perspective. And the permission to lead from a place that is fully yours.

Your detour didn't disqualify you.

It's pointing you to something deeper.

I'll meet you there.

A Note on Names and Privacy

This is a true story.

The events in this book are drawn from my lived experience and the lessons I've learned along the detour of leadership. Where possible, I've done my best to honor the spirit and emotional truth of each moment, while also protecting the privacy of others.

Some names and identifying details have been changed—particularly for coaching clients, colleagues, and individuals whose stories are intertwined with mine in sensitive or professional contexts.

For those whose names I chose to keep, especially those who influenced, supported, or shaped my journey in meaningful ways—thank you. Your impact lives on in these pages.

This book is a tribute to truth, not exposure.

A story of becoming, not blame.

Part I:
Foundations of Leadership

Chapter 1
Where I Started

The Power of Beginnings

Leadership lessons often begin long before we realize we are learning them—not in boardrooms, not in formal evaluations—but in the quiet spaces, the hard places—the moments no one else sees.

For me, those early lessons weren't wrapped in fancy titles or professional development seminars. They came from watching people navigate broken systems with unshakable dignity. They came from the way my guardian, Barbara Jackson, moved through the world—always with purpose, always with power, even when resources were scarce.

I didn't grow up surrounded by conventional symbols of success. There were no corner offices, no vision boards, no executives in tailored suits. What I saw instead were women who led without apology and without permission—who led with grit, with grace, and with strategies shaped by survival.

Chapter 1

In those early years, I didn't know I was studying leadership. I just knew I was watching something important—something real.

As I reflect on where I am today—as a coach, a strategist, a woman committed to helping others unlock their own power—I see clearly that every ounce of wisdom I offer now was seeded in those beginnings.

Beginnings matter. Not because they define us, but because they reveal who we are before the world tells us who to become.

Before I walk you through the big moments in my leadership story—before titles, promotions, and pivots—I want to start at the root.

That's where the real transformation begins.

Two Visions of Leadership

I had two very different perceptions of leadership growing up. On one hand, I saw the traditional images portrayed on television—men in suits, commanding rooms, making decisions that changed the world. On the other hand, I saw Barbara—armed not with a degree or title—leading with conviction, wisdom, and a fierce determination to fight for her community.

Barbara only completed what was considered an elementary education at the time—possibly up to eighth grade—but I have yet to meet anyone who could match her intellect or strategic thinking. She was clever, resourceful, and deeply rooted in justice. When we moved into the St. Thomas Housing Development—a government housing complex in New Orleans—it was as if her leadership instincts were ignited. She quickly became a key figure in resident-led efforts to improve living conditions in public housing.

It was the early 1980s in New Orleans—a city both vibrant and deeply divided, where public housing developments dotted the landscape and poverty was often met with neglect. One of those developments was the St. Thomas Housing Development, where my family lived in a four-bedroom apartment in what was called the Lower Garden District.

Chapter 1

Conditions had become unbearable. Apartments were deteriorating, utility bills were outrageously high, and basic repairs were being ignored. People were getting sick. Where most saw a broken system, Barbara Jackson saw an opportunity for collective action. Alongside her friend and fellow resident Fannie McKnight, Barbara led a historic year-long rent strike against the Housing Authority of New Orleans (HANO) in 1982.

What began as frustration quickly turned into organized resistance. These two women—neither of whom had formal education or traditional leadership roles—organized tenants with surgical precision. They established an escrow account so that residents could safely withhold rent without facing eviction, collected money orders from tenants, and kept detailed records of every transaction. The strike ultimately ended with HANO agreeing to modernize apartments and reduce utility fees—a win for the entire community. According to a 2014 article in The Times-Picayune, this strike remains one of the most successful resident-led movements in the city's public housing history.

Barbara didn't stop there. She continued to advocate for better housing, community policing, and tenant rights, eventually becoming president of the St. Thomas Resident Council. She had an uncanny ability to cut through chaos and make sense of complex systems. As one community leader put it, "Barbara was a brilliant strategist. She could stand in the middle of noise and chaos and make sense of it."

As a child, I didn't have the language to describe what I was seeing. I just knew it was powerful. I watched Barbara hold meetings, speak truth to power, and rally our neighbors. I often helped her write memos and letters, or document her thoughts for upcoming meetings. Without knowing it, I was getting my first lessons in leadership, advocacy, and the importance of using your voice.

I can still see it vividly—me, sitting on the floor of the St. Thomas Resident Council office, legs tucked underneath me, a notebook in hand, pretending to do homework while soaking everything in. I was always observing, always studying people. Even then, I was fascinated by body language and unspoken

Chapter 1

cues, watching how people showed up, how they negotiated space and power.

The women of the Resident Council would gather around the table, papers everywhere, conversations flying. And then there was Barbara—scribbling thoughts and strategy on whatever scrap of paper she could find. The funny thing was, nobody could ever make sense of what she'd written. Her notes looked like a secret code, full of arrows, shorthand, and phrases only she could decipher. It became a running joke that she was writing in another language and needed a translator.

Except…I could read it. Somehow, I always understood what she meant. One afternoon, in the middle of planning for a community meeting, Barbara looked up from her scribbles, waved the paper in the air, and with that thick, glorious Southern accent, said, "Here go my interpreter—Baabae, come write this for me."

The room laughed. I beamed. I stood beside her, heart racing with pride, and took the paper from her hands. "Tell me what you wanted to say," I asked.

She'd walk me through her thoughts, and I'd shape them into clear sentences. I wasn't just transcribing—I was translating her brilliance into something others could receive. She trusted me. She gave me a role. And more than anything, she gave me the confidence to believe that my words—and my voice—had value.

Reflection

That moment planted a seed in me: that leadership isn't about titles or speaking the loudest. Sometimes, it's about listening deeply, translating vision into action, and helping others find the words to match their power.

Barbara Jackson: *The Servant Leader*

I didn't yet know the frameworks or theories, I just knew that Barbara led differently. She didn't demand attention—she earned it. She didn't seek power—she wielded it for others. Long before I ever heard the term servant leadership, I saw it lived out in the way she moved through the world.

Chapter 1

The term servant leadership was coined by Robert Greenleaf in the 1970s. He defined it as a philosophy where the leader's primary role is to serve—the team, the community, the people. It flips traditional models of leadership on their head. Instead of asking, "How can people serve the leader's vision?" the servant leader asks, "How can the leader serve the people's needs and elevate their potential?"

Barbara embodied every tenet of this framework without ever stepping foot into a formal leadership course. She:

- Centered the needs of the community before her own comfort
- Made decisions rooted in collective well-being
- Listened first, acted second
- Developed others by inviting them into the process
- Built trust through consistency and integrity

When she led the rent strike, she wasn't doing it to elevate herself—she was doing it to make sure children didn't grow up in mold-ridden apartments, that elders had safe water, that families could thrive.

Her leadership was practical, spiritual, and strategic all at once.

As I grew older and began studying leadership models in a professional context, I was stunned by how many theories echoed what Barbara already knew: that leadership is about lifting others, not elevating yourself. That power is not a possession—it's a responsibility.

Even now, when I coach executives who are navigating organizational politics or culture change, I find myself drawing from Barbara's blueprint. I often ask my clients:

- Are you leading to be seen, or to create visibility for others?
- Are you building trust, or simply building compliance?
- Are you making space for others to rise—or are you standing in the center too long?

Barbara never asked those questions out loud. But her life answered them every single day.

Looking back, I realize that the first model of leadership I ever studied didn't come from a

Chapter 1

textbook—it came from Barbara's kitchen table.

Leadership in Action: *Barbara Among Giants*

It wasn't just what Barbara did—it was how she did it. One of her greatest strengths was knowing how to bring out the best in others, even when their approaches were wildly different from hers.

Take Fannie McKnight—"McKnight," as Barbara always called her. McKnight didn't walk into a room — she stormed in. Always with her bullhorn, always ready for a fight, her voice could carry across the entire housing development. She shot from the hip, full of righteous fury, and her passion was magnetic. She had a roar in her spirit that refused to be silenced. If someone wasn't doing their job, McKnight would let them know—on the spot, with no sugarcoating.

Barbara, on the other hand, was calm, steady. She didn't shout—she strategized. And yet, the only person who could calm McKnight when she was mid-roar was Barbara. I watched it happen time and time again. During one particularly tense planning meeting ahead of a sit-down with HANO, McKnight was hyping the team up, stomping around the room, firing off demands.

Barbara let her go for a while. Then, right before the meeting began, she placed a gentle hand on McKnight's arm and said, "Now McKnight, you gon' speak—save that fire for when it'll hit hardest. Let's get them talking first. Let 'em think they got the upper hand." And McKnight listened.

Barbara knew exactly when McKnight's fire was needed—and how to shape it so that it burned strategically and not just hot.

Then there was Mrs. Carol Steward. The opposite of McKnight in every way. Soft-spoken, always smiling, her voice rarely rose above a whisper. Because she spoke so rarely, when she did talk, everyone leaned in. She didn't demand attention—she commanded it, simply by being intentional with her words.

Barbara understood the rhythm of both women. She never tried to make McKnight quieter or Carol louder. Instead, she orchestrated space for both.

Chapter 1

She'd guide the conversation like a conductor—letting McKnight stir urgency, letting Carol anchor reflection, and stepping in herself to connect it all back to the goal.

That day I mentioned earlier—when the HANO official came to meet with the Council—Barbara had everyone ready. McKnight had rallied the room, Carol would close with a quiet yet powerful appeal, and Barbara, as always, would tie it all together. The result? Unified, undeniable, unstoppable.

That day, I learned something that would stay with me forever: leadership isn't just about vision—it's also about timing, temperament, and trust. The ability to bring different voices into harmony is what makes a leader unforgettable.

What I Now Teach, Barbara Lived

The models I coach executives through today are the same principles I first saw—unlabeled, unspoken—through Barbara's actions. Here's how her natural brilliance aligns with three modern leadership frameworks:

Where I Started

Barbara's Legacy:
Where Leadership Meets Life

① SERVANT LEADERSHIP

"The leader exists to serve first."
– Robert Greenleaf

Barbara's Example:

She organized for the betterment of the community, not for status or recognition. She listened deeply, protected the most vulnerable, and made decisions rooted in people—not ego.

What I Coach Now:

Leaders must ask themselves:

Whose needs am I centering?

Am I building followers—or more leaders?

② ADAPTIVE LEADERSHIP

"Leadership is about helping people tackle tough challenges and thrive."
– Heifetz & Linsky

Barbara's Example:

Faced with a broken housing system, she didn't wait for permission—she led through the unknown, mobilized collective problem-solving, and adjusted strategies in real time.

What I Coach Now:

Great leaders build resilience by helping others manage change, uncertainty, and the discomfort of doing things differently.

③ EMOTIONAL INTELLIGENCE (EQ)

"Emotions drive behavior. Awareness drives leadership."

– Daniel Goleman

Barbara's Example:

Though she was firm and direct, she connected with people through empathy and intuition. I watched her calm a room with a look, and persuade without raising her voice.

What I Coach Now:

Executive presence starts with self-awareness and relational awareness. Leaders must learn to read the room, regulate their own emotions, and connect beyond authority.

Where I Started

 **Coaching Prompt**

Which of these leadership approaches—*servant leadership, adaptive leadership,* or *emotional intelligence*—do you currently embody most? Which one do you need to strengthen to lead more powerfully?

Dream vs. Reality

Growing up in the St. Thomas Housing Development meant growing up with a very narrow window into what was possible. Dreams always felt... distant. Not because we didn't dream, but because the world around us rarely reflected those dreams back to us as something real or attainable. It was as if dreams belonged to people in other zip codes, in homes with lawns and bookshelves and bedtime stories. Our community, though rich in love, culture, and resilience, wasn't built for dreaming big—it was built for surviving.

Chapter 1

From an early age, I understood I was different. School came naturally to me. I loved learning from the moment I stepped foot into a classroom. The only reason I ever made it into that classroom was because child welfare intervened. My birth mother, Josephine, had kept me home well past the typical starting age. When the authorities got involved, she had no choice but to enroll me. I was nearly two years behind, and I had to repeat the first grade.

Somewhere between that first and second year of first grade, I went to live with Barbara. I don't remember exactly when—those details blur—but I remember the shift. Barbara stepped in not just as a guardian, but as a guide. She enrolled me in school, structured my world, and began to shape the foundation I would stand on for years to come.

Thinking back, I didn't mind repeating first grade. I also didn't fully understand what "repeating" meant —I just knew I loved school. I still remember my first teacher, Ms. Clapion. She was kind and brilliant and made me feel like I belonged. It's funny—I don't have a lot of vivid memories from that part of my life.

Still, I remember every single one of my grade school teachers. They were all extraordinary. They saw something in me, and I felt seen.

By fourth grade, I was tested and placed in the gifted program. The school even proposed skipping me ahead a couple of grades to make up for the time I'd lost. I was elated. The idea of new books, more challenging work, and sitting with older students felt like an adventure waiting to happen.

Barbara said no.

Isn't it strange how certain conversations stay with you, even when everything else fades? This was one of those moments. We were sitting at the kitchen table, and I could hardly contain my excitement. She listened carefully, then said, "They ain't telling me nothing I don't already know. A blind man can see how smart you are…in books, that is." She paused. "However, I don't think you're ready to be with the older children. You're still young in the mind."

I didn't understand it then. I was hurt, even a little angry. It felt like she was holding me back. But instead of letting me skip grades, she made sure I was

Chapter 1

enrolled in the Academic Enrichment Program (AEP), where I could be challenged without being pushed too far, too fast.

That program quenched my thirst for deeper learning. It didn't just offer harder assignments; it affirmed that I belonged in a space of excellence. I loved it so much that when we later moved into the St. Thomas Housing Development, I begged Barbara not to make me transfer to the neighborhood school. And again—she showed up for me.

She petitioned the school board to let me remain at McDonogh #36, and once approved, I began commuting by city bus—two each way. The school district covered part of the fare, not the full trip. If Barbara didn't have the twenty-five cents I needed for a transfer, I'd ride the first bus and walk the rest of the way. Rain or shine. Morning and evening. Because that classroom fed me in ways I didn't yet know how to explain.

Now, I see the wisdom in Barbara's decision. She wasn't questioning my intelligence—she was protecting my development. She knew the world wouldn't be kind to a little Black girl who was academically advanced—yet emotionally unprepared. She was thinking ahead in a way I couldn't at the time. She was shaping me not just to succeed—but to survive and thrive in a world that would not hand me anything easily.

Lesson

Intelligence opens doors, but emotional readiness allows you to walk through them with confidence. Barbara's decision taught me that leadership is not just about what you can do—it's about knowing when and how you're ready to do it.

That decision, though difficult for me to accept at the time, planted the seeds for one of the most important leadership qualities I would come to understand: self-awareness. I was beginning to learn who I was—not just what I could do academically, but how I navigated the world emotionally, socially,

Chapter 1

and intuitively. Barbara saw beyond my potential and into my readiness. And in doing so, she gave me the gift of time—the time to grow into myself.

The Power of Self-Awareness

By middle school, I began to fully embrace my academic identity. Every awards day, I walked home with a stack of certificates, ribbons, and recognition. It became my thing—the one area where I consistently excelled. In a world that didn't always offer affirmation freely, school became the space where I knew I would shine. It wasn't just about grades. It was about being seen.

During this time, I didn't have many material possessions. I didn't have the newest clothes or the latest toys. But I had my intellect. And I held onto that like it was gold. Not because I wanted to prove anything to anyone—but because it was the one thing no one could take from me.

And I was aware of it. Not boastfully—because it was always affirmed. Teachers praised me. Classmates looked to me for help. Barbara expecting nothing less than excellence. If I came home with anything less than an "A," I had to explain it. She wasn't being harsh —she knew what I was capable of and she wouldn't let me play small.

Even in the midst of all that success, I had my own quiet battles. I remember one classmate in particular —let's call her Genie. Genie and I were in the same classes from fourth through sixth grade. She was beautiful, light-skinned with long hair always parted into perfect ponytails, her outfits flawless every single day. In my community at the time, people referred to her complexion as "high yella"—a term I now recognize as harsh and rooted in colorism. Back then, it was just part of the language we absorbed.

Genie wasn't just pretty—she was also brilliant. Grade for grade, she matched me. As much as I didn't want to admit it at the time, I saw her as my competition. I didn't like her. She hadn't done anything to me. It was because she represented everything I didn't think I had. She had poise, polish, and presence. Instead of admiring her, I acted out. I pulled her ponytails. I

Chapter 1

picked at her. I was mean to her—for no reason other than my own insecurity.

After one awards day—where, as usual, Genie and I had both cleaned up—I was standing with Barbara when Genie's mom approached us. My heart sank. I just knew she was about to scold me for how I treated her daughter. Instead, she extended her hand to me, smiled, and congratulated me. Then she turned to Barbara and said something I'll never forget:

"Would it be okay if she came over to study with Genie after school? They're both so smart—I think they'd do well together."

I was stunned. Had Genie not told her mom? Or...had she told her, and this was her mom's way of resolving it—gracefully, without shame? Did she see through my meanness and recognize it for what it really was: envy, insecurity, the awkward expression of a girl who didn't yet know how to handle someone who mirrored her ambition and beauty? I didn't know. What I did know was that her mom was kind to me— genuinely kind. That kindness disarmed me more than any confrontation ever could.

Barbara, always encouraging of anything that would help me grow, didn't hesitate. "Of course," she said. "I need her to be around other smart kids."

Just like that, Genie and I became best friends for the next year or so. We studied together. We pushed each other. Slowly, I stopped seeing her as competition and started seeing her as a mirror—one that reflected back what I was capable of becoming—not what I lacked.

Looking back, I realize Genie was the first person who taught me how easily insecurity can disguise itself as conflict. I had mistaken her excellence for a threat, when in fact, it was an invitation—to rise, to expand, to confront parts of myself I hadn't yet claimed.

It was one of my earliest lessons in emotional intelligence, even though I wouldn't have used those words back then. Genie never did anything to harm me. She wasn't arrogant. She didn't boast. But the way she moved—the ease with which she carried herself, the admiration she received—exposed something raw in me.

I hadn't yet learned how to sit with that discomfort, to ask what it was really pointing to.

That experience would shape how I approach leadership to this day.

Now, when I coach executives navigating tension with a peer or colleague, I often ask them to pause—not to defend or deflect— to dig.

- What story are you telling yourself about that person?
- Where is the comparison clouding connection?
- What fear might be hiding behind your frustration?

Insecure leadership isn't always loud. Sometimes, it's silent sabotage—the quiet dismissal of others' gifts, the internal competition no one else knows about and the score you're keeping. Awareness changes everything. When we name our patterns, we reclaim our power.

That season in my life revealed that self-awareness isn't just about knowing your strengths—it's about recognizing the fears and insecurities that live beside them. It's about being open to connection, even with the people who trigger our discomfort.

Years later, in my professional career, I found myself navigating the same dynamic—only this time, I wasn't the insecure one. I was the rising star.

I had entered a role that came with visibility, expectations, and a long shadow cast by leaders who had held power for years. I was confident in my skills, even as I was still learning how to navigate systems that didn't always welcome new energy—especially not from someone like me. As I stepped into leadership, I began to notice the same unspoken

> **Self-awareness** is the foundation of leadership. It's the quiet voice that reminds you who you are, even when the world doesn't reflect it back to you. It's what helps you name your power—and own your shadow. It's what gives you permission to take up space, and grace to make space for others too.

Chapter 1

tension I had once projected onto Genie—only now, I was on the receiving end.

There were meetings where my ideas were dismissed until they came from someone else. Invitations that never made it to my calendar. Feedback that felt more like control than support. I'd watch seasoned leaders shift in their chairs when I spoke—small tells of discomfort that echoed the silent rivalries I remembered from grade school.

At first, I took it personally. Then I remembered Genie. I remembered what it felt like to see someone's light and feel threatened by it. And I realized—some of these senior leaders weren't reacting to me. They were reacting to what my presence represented—change, evolution, and the uncomfortable truth that their way of leading wasn't the only way anymore.

It was a sobering realization, and also a freeing one. Their insecurities had nothing to do with my worth—and everything to do with their own fear of being eclipsed.

Now, when I coach high-potential leaders who find

themselves in similar situations, I remind them of this: sometimes resistance isn't about your readiness—it's about their insecurity. Your job isn't to shrink. It's to stay grounded in your growth and lead anyway.

You can't control how others receive your light. You can choose not to dim it.

Coaching Prompt

Self-awareness is more than recognizing your strengths. It's about becoming intimately familiar with how those strengths show up—and what insecurities or habits may be attached to them. It's also about being honest about the stories we've told ourselves about others, and how those stories may have masked our own growth opportunities.

Chapter 1

Reflection

Take a moment to reflect on your early experiences:

- Who was the "Genie" in your life—someone you saw as a rival, but who may have actually been a mirror for your own growth?
- What insecurities lived beside your strengths in childhood or early adulthood?
- Can you recall a time when someone saw something in you—even when you weren't showing up at your best?
- How did your environment shape how you expressed or hid your strengths?

Closing Thoughts

Your leadership journey didn't begin with a job title or a performance review.

Mine certainly didn't.

Mine started in the smallest moments—sitting cross-legged on the floor of the Resident Council office, pretending to do homework while brilliant women strategized over community policy.

It began when someone saw my potential but also protected my pace.

It emerged when I mistook someone's strength for a threat—only to realize later that she was a mirror, not a rival.

It was shaped by every early affirmation, every dawn bus ride, every moment I used my voice before I even knew how powerful it could be.

It was shaped by how others responded to my light—and how I learned to protect it, even when it made them uncomfortable.

What I've come to understand is this: leadership isn't about arrival. It's about awareness. The more deeply we know ourselves, the more powerfully we can lead others.

Whether you're just beginning your leadership path or stepping into a new season of growth, don't overlook the early moments. Don't dismiss the silent lessons. The truth is—your story has been preparing you to lead all along.

Chapter 1

Rooted leaders grow stronger. Self-aware leaders rise further. And the best leaders? We don't wait for permission—we lead from the lessons that shaped us, even the ones we didn't ask for.

Before you rush forward, pause. Take a look back. That's where your clarity begins.

> **Want to Go Deeper?**
>
> If Chapter 1 sparked something in you, you're not alone. I created a Companion Guide to help you turn these insights into action.
>
> Inside Chapter 1 of the guide, you'll find:
>
> - Guided journal prompts to explore your own early leadership lessons
> - Exercises to unpack how your origin story shapes how you lead
> - Space to reflect, reset, and root yourself in self-awareness
>
> This guide is available for purchase at
> www.diamondconsultantsllc.com
>
>

Because leadership starts with clarity.
And clarity starts here.

Chapter 2
Lessons in Belonging

"I had spent years learning how to lead—however, no one had prepared me for the cost of constantly questioning whether I belonged in the rooms I had worked so hard to enter."

—Dr. Tammi Fleming

The Many Faces of Belonging

Belonging isn't always about being welcomed. Sometimes it's about surviving. Sometimes it's about being quiet long enough to stay in the room. For a Southern Black woman navigating professional spaces in the North, it often meant translating my whole self, not just my words.

I've spent a lifetime managing the weight of multiple "isms." Racism. Sexism. Classism. In my early years, growing up in the South, these systems weren't subtle—they were bold, present, and predictable. You could feel them in the air. You knew where you stood. The lines were visible. That didn't make them easier— it did make them clearer.

When I moved North and began entering professional environments, the boundaries blurred. The acts of exclusion weren't loud or obvious—they were hidden in tone, in glances, in the kinds of questions that sounded curious, yet cut deep. The moments that made me wonder, *Was that about me? Or am I imagining things?*

Rooted in Southern Rhythm

In the South, I grew up with language and culture that felt familiar and right. I said "icebox" instead of refrigerator. "Cold drink" instead of soda. These weren't just words—they were the music of my upbringing, the rhythm of my roots. I didn't just speak—I sang, in the way Southern Black folks do when storytelling is both a gift and a survival tool.

Over the years, I've often been complimented on the rhythm of my voice—its musicality, its warmth, its depth. People have asked if I'm from an island, and I always smile and say, "Yes—the island of New Orleans. And on some days, maybe St. Thomas, too." It wasn't until later in life that I realized what they were hearing wasn't foreign—it was the rich blend of Southern cadence, inner-city linguistics, and Afrocentric storytelling passed down through generations.

That rhythm is more than regional—it's ancestral. It's the griot tradition. It's the oral history embedded in my bones. It's how we made sense of a
world that didn't always make room for us in books or boardrooms. While I now understand its power, for many years I tried to hide it.

I softened my accent in meetings. I carefully reworded my thoughts to sound more "professional." I shortened stories that once would've stretched beautifully across a porch conversation. I code-switched in words, tempo, tone, and timing. The easiest parts to edit were my clothes or hair—the harder edits were internal. I filtered my full self so I could remain palatable in spaces that didn't know how to receive me.

Yet, what makes us uniquely American is the fact that we are all uniquely different. Bringing those differences—our voice, our rhythm, our stories—into professional spaces is not a weakness. It's a benefit. I didn't always believe that. I had to unlearn years of performing belonging before I could reclaim it.

That performance wasn't limited to language. It lived in the fabric of how I showed up—literally.

When I first moved to Philadelphia from New Orleans, I had just entered a new income bracket. I was proud, independent, and still carried the vibrant style of the community that raised me. Bright neon outfits, loud colors, bold prints. My wardrobe wasn't just fashion—it was a celebration. It said, I'm here. I've arrived. I belong.

One morning, I stepped into the office feeling radiant—confident in a bright ensemble that reminded me of home. As I poured my coffee, a younger white colleague turned to me and asked, "Why do you always wear such bright colors?" It was framed as curiosity, yet I heard the judgment in her tone. My heart dropped. I felt so good that morning. I thought I looked beautiful. But in an instant, I was questioning whether my presence—my joy—was too much.

I smiled and brushed it off with a lighthearted joke: "I dress to match my emotions. I was feeling pretty bright today." We both laughed. Still, something in me shifted. I started shopping differently, more neutrals, more blacks, browns, and navy blues. Slowly, my style began to fade into the background. And with it, my voice began to dim—not from shame of my roots, but from fear that being too bold would mean being overlooked.

 ## Reflection

Looking back, it's hard to explain how something so small—a single comment, a passing question—could ripple so deeply. But that's the nature of microaggressions. They don't shout; they whisper. They wrap themselves in politeness and curiosity— underneath is a message: You're different.

Chapter 2

> You don't quite fit. And when you hear that message enough times in enough subtle ways, you begin to do the work for them. You quiet yourself before anyone asks. You blend before anyone stares. You shrink before anyone tells you to shrink.

The Subtle Shifts

As my wardrobe faded, so did parts of my presence. I didn't love color less—I feared being seen too much.

Over time, those subtle shifts became a strategy. A survival mechanism. I wasn't just trying to fit in—I was trying to be less noticeable, less misunderstood, less misread. I wasn't trying to disappear— I was trying to disturb the room less.

That's the tricky part. The shifts didn't happen all at once. They happened gradually, quietly. So quietly, I didn't even realize how much of myself I was leaving behind until I began to feel disconnected from the very woman I had fought so hard to become.

I don't think change is inherently wrong. We all evolve. Some of that evolution is natural, even beautiful. But many of my shifts weren't born from personal expression—they were born from survival, from a desire to fit into rooms that were not made with me in mind.

Classism, like racism and sexism, knows how to dress up. It wears blazers and boardroom etiquette. It doesn't call you poor—it questions whether your lunch is "too strong" or whether your shoes are "appropriate for the event." It shows up in makeup conversations, in side-eyes about natural hair, in raised eyebrows when someone uses a colloquialism not found in a corporate style guide. It's the assumption that professionalism looks one way, sounds one way, and definitely doesn't wear hoop earrings.

I adapted. Not because I lacked confidence—but because I had been conditioned to believe that being fully myself might close more doors than it opened. I wanted to be taken seriously. I wanted to move up. I wanted to prove that I belonged.

What I didn't realize was that the more I edited myself to match the room, the more disconnected I became from the wisdom, warmth, and brilliance that got me into the room in the first place.

The problem with shrinking is that it doesn't just make you smaller to others—it makes you smaller to yourself. Your words get quieter. Your instincts feel less trustworthy. Your brilliance, once bright and unfiltered, becomes wrapped in hesitation.

Yet, no one ever says, "You're allowed to stop now." You just keep adjusting. Keep translating. Keep folding pieces of yourself into corners so no one is uncomfortable.

Until one day, you're the one who's uncomfortable in your own skin.

The Psychology and Politics of Belonging

It took me years to understand the difference between belonging and fitting in.

I used to think they were the same. I thought if I

could just learn the norms, follow the rules, and mirror the room, I'd eventually feel at home. But that feeling never came. And it wasn't because I wasn't trying hard enough—it was because I was trying too hard to become someone I wasn't.

Brené Brown once said, "True belonging doesn't require you to change who you are. It requires you to be who you are." When I first heard that, it hit me like a truth I had already lived, yet never named.

For years, I had been fitting in. I had been performing a version of myself that others could accept. I had worn the right outfits, softened the accent, skipped the stories, and streamlined the soul. I wasn't showing up fully—I was showing up safely.

Then, I encountered the work of john a. powell, who speaks about individual belonging and goes beyond those boundaries and explains systems of othering. He writes about how institutions are designed to include some and exclude others—with policies and with culture. His words gave shape to something I'd felt, even though I couldn't articulate it: that I wasn't just experiencing moments of exclusion—I was navigating a structure that had never really expected me to belong.

According to powell, belonging is not just about inclusion—it's about power. Who defines the culture? Who sets the norms? Who holds the mic when we talk about what's "professional," what's "appropriate," what's "good leadership"?

The questions made me realize something hard and freeing at the same time: I wasn't failing at belonging. I was resisting erasure.

Because the truth is, you can't belong in a space that only welcomes edited versions of you.

Belonging is not about being accepted. **It's about being unchanged by acceptance.**

Professionalism or Performance?

Professionalism, I learned, isn't neutral—it's coded. It had a tone, a look, a rhythm that didn't match mine. It meant being assertive—but never loud. Stylish—but never bold. Confident—but never too Southern. It meant constant translation—and being praised for how well you did it.

But here's the thing: code-switching is not just about language. It's about legibility—making yourself readable to those in power. And it's often about survival, not preference.

Historically, what we now call "professional" was defined in boardrooms where only one kind of person was allowed to belong. Those standards weren't created for me—they were created without me. And for a long time, I thought I had to master them to matter.

I thought assimilation was the path to advancement. Over time, I realized: **Assimilation without authenticity is erasure.**

It was never just about being excellent. It was about being excellent in a way that didn't make anyone uncomfortable. That meant trimming parts of myself that were never a threat to begin with—they were just unfamiliar.

That's when I began to see the cost of that kind of professionalism. Not just to me—to the culture of the organizations where I worked.

When everyone starts looking, sounding, and leading the same, something precious gets lost: Perspective. Innovation. Truth.

I started to wonder: If I have to erase myself to succeed here—what exactly am I succeeding at?

The Push and Pull

There's a tension I've carried for much of my life—the weight of being in between.

I worked tirelessly to enter spaces that once felt unreachable. I earned my way in. I showed up prepared, credentialed, and committed. Once I arrived, I often found that the room wasn't ready for me—or rather, it wasn't built with me in mind.

So, the push began: to adjust, to adapt, to translate myself into something more palatable. That was the price of staying.

Just as I was pushing to fit into those new rooms, something else was happening. I was being pulled away from the places I came from. The community where I once felt at home began to feel distant. My language shifted. My wardrobe changed. My time was no longer my own. My success, while deeply earned, sometimes created a quiet wedge between me and the people who once knew me best.

I was too much for one world and not enough for another—always editing, always adjusting, always trying to calibrate just the right version of myself to feel acceptable in either place.

This wasn't just cultural code-switching—it was emotional dislocation. It wasn't just about being misunderstood by others. It was about becoming unfamiliar to myself.

That's the part no one prepares you for.

The guilt of walking into your old neighborhood and wondering if you've become someone else. The sadness of being surrounded by success and still feeling invisible. The ache of realizing that the version of you they celebrate in the boardroom is a fraction of the one your guardian raised.

Chapter 2

It's a strange kind of displacement—not of geography—but of identity. A sense that you no longer fully belong anywhere. That the very progress you worked for is now isolating you. That in becoming "successful," you've become unrecognizable—to others, and sometimes, to yourself.

And in that in-between space—where you're never quite enough, and always a little too much—imposter syndrome finds fertile ground. Not because you're a fraud, but because you've been rewarded more for adjusting than for being.

This tension, painful as it is, became my teacher. It taught me to ask better questions:

- What parts of me am I shrinking to stay in this room?
- Who told me I had to?
- What would it cost me to stop?

It taught me that belonging isn't just about being accepted by others. It's about refusing to abandon yourself.

Imposter Syndrome

That in-between space—the one where you're constantly adjusting, constantly performing—is where imposter syndrome often takes root. It doesn't arrive all at once. It creeps in quietly, disguised as humility, masked as professionalism. But what it really is... is doubt—deep, chronic, internalized doubt.

When you've spent years hearing—directly or indirectly—that your voice is too loud, your style too bold, your background too different, it becomes easy to internalize the idea that you're not enough. Or worse, that you're too much. Even when you've earned your place, the question lingers: Did I really? Or did I just slip through before someone noticed?

> ***Imposter Syndrome*** involves persistent feelings of self-doubt and perceived fraudulence, even in the face of evidence that you are skilled, accomplished, and competent. According to the American Psychological Association, it can lead high-achieving individuals to downplay their success, attributing it to luck, timing or external help rather than their own ability or preparation.
>
> Source: American Psychological Association

Chapter 2

That question follows you. It follows you into meetings, where you rehearse your thoughts before speaking. It follows you into decision-making, where you second-guess your instincts. It follows you into your leadership, where you shrink even as others look to you for strength.

You start seeking validation for what you already know—apologizing for taking up space. And the most heartbreaking part? You begin to distrust your own brilliance. You dim the very light that made people notice you in the first place.

Here's what I've come to know: imposter syndrome doesn't mean you don't belong. It means you've been made to feel that you have to earn belonging over and over again. That's not your burden to carry.

Arriving in Belonging

Now, at 53, I no longer ask for permission to belong. I've stopped performing, stopped softening, stopped offering only the pieces of myself that others can easily digest.

Belonging, I've learned, isn't something you wait to be granted—it's something you choose to reclaim.

For me, that reclamation has come in waves. It's in the way my Southern accent now flows freely when I feel safe. In the warmth of my words, the rhythm of my speech, the unapologetic cadence of a woman who has learned to love her voice again. As I reflect on consistent reactions during public or intimate speaking engagements. Remember what I said about people thinking I sound like I'm from the islands? It still makes me smile–because in a way, I am. The island of New Orleans. The roots of the Gulf. The rhythm of a people who've always made music from struggle, style from scarcity, and strength from story.

These days, if you hear my accent, consider it a gift. It means I'm at ease. It means I'm home in myself. It's a sign that I'm not guarding my words—or my heart.

Belonging, for me, is not about fitting into a system that was never built with me in mind. It's about honoring the parts of me I used to hide. The language. The style. The story. The edge. It's about letting my full self into the room—even if the room shifts a little when I do.

Because real belonging doesn't require performance. It invites presence. It's not about being perfect—it's about being whole.

As I've grown, I've realized: I don't need to fit in to lead. I need to be aligned to lead—with my values, my stories, my voice. That's where my power lives. Not in assimilation, but in authenticity.

Imposter Syndrome in Real Time:
A Conversation with Regina

As I was reviewing this chapter, I had a powerful conversation with my colleague and friend Regina. We were reflecting on imposter syndrome—not just as a concept—but as a lived experience. She brought up a memory I had nearly forgotten: the time I recommended her for a high-profile contract.

"You believed in me before I did," she said.

She told me what I didn't know back then. How the voice in her head wasn't saying, *"You can't do this,"*—it was saying, "*You have to be perfect, every deliverable, every communication, every step.*" The pressure of perfection wasn't motivating—it was paralyzing. To others, it looked like she wasn't following up. But inside, she was frozen by a constant, gnawing fear that she wouldn't be good enough.

She reflected on how bad she felt about not moving forward. How she worried it made me look bad. I remembered calling her—gently asking, "Hey, what's going on with the project?" I didn't accuse. I didn't pressure. But I sensed something deeper.

What I didn't say then—but shared during our conversation—was that my intuition told me it wasn't about the project at all. I recognized that hesitation because I had lived it. I had also second-guessed myself, hidden behind over-preparedness, or waited for the "right moment" that never came.

After that project, I shifted my approach. I stopped asking, "Did you finish it?" and started saying, "Where are you on it—and can we work through it together?" Sometimes it was just enough to help her get unstuck, to thaw the freeze that perfectionism had created.

As our conversation deepened, we began naming what we had both experienced—how imposter syndrome isn't always loud or obvious. It doesn't always sound like "I'm not good enough." Sometimes it's more subtle. More familiar. It sounds like, "You should wait," or "You're not quite ready," or "If this isn't perfect, they'll regret giving you the chance."

Regina told me how much she appreciated that I never made her feel ashamed. That I helped her move without ever naming the thing. Now, with more language and reflection, she could name it. "I didn't know what it was back then," she said. "But now I do. That was imposter syndrome."

And it was. But it didn't look like mine.

That's the thing. Imposter syndrome doesn't have one face. Sometimes it over-functions. Sometimes it freezes. Sometimes it silences. Sometimes it over-explains. Once you know how to see it in yourself, you begin to recognize it in others.

The real work is learning not just how to push through it—but how to **hold space** for someone else who's caught in it. And maybe even whisper back: **"I see you. I've been there. Let's move through it—together."**

Because your belonging doesn't live in their approval. It lives in your decision to bring your full self to the table—and to trust that doing so is more than brave. It's necessary.

Coaching Prompt

Take a moment to think about a time when you questioned whether you truly belonged in a room you had every right to be in.

- What triggered that feeling?
- What did your body do—your posture, your voice, your presence?
- Did you shrink to stay?

Now imagine walking into that same space today—not seeking approval, not hoping to be accepted. Just knowing that your

presence has value just as it is.
- Where have you edited or erased parts of yourself to be accepted?
- What part of your identity are you ready to reclaim?
- What would it look like to lead from your whole self instead of your most "acceptable" version?

Today, when I coach leaders—especially those navigating spaces where they feel unseen, out of place, or underestimated—I start with the very lessons I had to learn the hard way.

I teach that **authenticity is not a liability**. It's not a weakness to be managed—it's a superpower to be harnessed. The voice you were once told to quiet is often the one the room most needs to hear. The parts of you, you were trained to tuck away are often the most potent tools you have as a leader.

In my sessions, I invite clients to identify the pieces of themselves they've put away just to survive—then challenge them to consider: What would leadership look like if you brought those pieces back?

Because leadership isn't about perfectly performing what others expect. It's about standing in what you know, even when your knowing looks or sounds different from theirs.

True leadership doesn't begin when you lead from your edits—it begins when you lead from your essence.

The Emotional Cost of Belonging

No one tells you how tiring it is to make yourself belong.

They celebrate your poise, your polish, your professionalism. They don't see the layers underneath. The mental math you're doing in every conversation. The self-monitoring. The rehearsals. The silences. The smiles that say, I'm fine, even when your spirit is worn out from bending.

Belonging—when it's built on adjustment rather than acceptance—is not a blessing. It's a burden.

And it is exhausting!

It's the kind of exhaustion that doesn't come from staying up late or working long hours. It comes from constantly calculating:

- Is this too much?
- Should I soften that?
- Do I sound too passionate? Too emotional? Too direct?
- Will this land? Or will it label me?

It's the kind of tired that makes you second-guess your joy, your edge, your laughter. That makes you over-apologize and under-celebrate. That makes you afraid to take up space—even when you've earned every inch of it.

I used to think I was tired from the work. Eventually, I realized: It wasn't the work that was draining me. It was the performance.

The constant toggling between who I am and who I need to be to be palatable. The fear that being fully myself might cost me respect, connection, or even opportunity. And the deeper fear that, if I stopped performing, I might disappear altogether.

Here's the truth most high-achieving women carry quietly:

We're not just burned out from doing too much.

We're burned out from being too little of ourselves for too long.

Because real belonging doesn't drain you.

It doesn't ask you to fracture your identity.

It doesn't reward you for invisibility.

Real belonging nourishes.

It gives back what the world so often asks you to give away—your wholeness, your energy, your joy.

Closing Thoughts

Belonging isn't about fitting into a mold.

It's about breaking the mold with your presence.

It's not something handed to you. It's something

Chapter 2

you decide—again and again—to stand in. To speak from. To lead with.

When you stop shrinking, stop apologizing, stop second-guessing the very brilliance that brought you to the table, you stop asking, "Do I belong here?"

And you start declaring:

"This space is better because I am here."

Want to Go Deeper?

If this chapter stirred something in you—if you've ever felt the tension of showing up edited, uncertain, or unseen—know that you're not alone. You don't have to untangle it alone either.

The Leadership Detour Companion Guide includes guided journal prompts, embodiment exercises, and practical tools to help you:

- *Identify the spaces where you've been shrinking,*
- *Reclaim the parts of your identity you've tucked away to survive,*
- *Begin building a leadership practice rooted in authenticity, not assimilation.*

You'll also find a special "Voice Reclamation" challenge and a visual exercise on what it means to lead without a mask.

Purchase your digital or print copy at
www.diamondconsultantsllc.com

Turn the page—your full presence belongs in every room you enter.

Chapter 3
The First Detour: The Gap Between Talent and Leadership

"I thought doing good work was enough. I was wrong."

—Dr. Tammi Fleming

The Gap Between Talent and Leadership

Imagine this: I'm 21 years old and just landed my first professional job as an administrative assistant at a small nonprofit. I'm young, eager, determined. I showed up early, stayed late, mastered the office systems, and quickly became the go-to person for everything from scheduling to grant reports. Within two years, I was promoted to Outreach Engagement Specialist.

From there, the momentum never really stopped—at least not at first. I kept climbing. Program Coordinator. Project Director. I moved from local organizations to regional ones, then to national platforms. I checked all the boxes. I took every training offered, mastered every tool, hit every metric. Even the occasional setbacks didn't slow me down for long. I always bounced back, often stronger.

For nearly two decades, I moved forward with clarity and confidence, fueled by my drive and sharpened by my experience. My title changed, my salary grew, and my influence expanded. I was doing exactly what I had been taught to do: work hard, stay sharp, be excellent. I was the high performer. The problem-solver. The dependable one.

Then, somewhere around forty, I hit a wall.

Not a sudden crash. A slow, almost imperceptible stall. I began to notice the shift. The opportunities I had once been sought out for began to pass me by. The growth I once took for granted slowed to a crawl. I looked around and saw colleagues being elevated, even though they didn't always have deeper experience or sharper skills. They brought something else to the table. Something I couldn't quite name.

Chapter 3

Despite all I had achieved, I felt like my career was regressing instead of progressing. I was frustrated, confused. I'd done everything right. Or so I thought.

But the clearest example of how deeply I had misunderstood the rules of the game came when I was transferred to a newly formed unit. On paper, we were equals—each of us reporting to a new VP who was tasked with shaping this team into something fresh and impactful. We were building something new together—ambitious, hopeful, uncertain.

I poured myself into the work. I managed a significant body of work, leveraged funding to scale impact, and positioned myself as someone willing to carry the load. I represented the team at agency-wide events, committees, and even social functions—often the only one in the room flying our flag. I took pride in building feedback loops, ensuring I brought the collective voice back to the table. I was stretching myself to lead without a title, believing it would speak for itself.

Then came the restructuring.

The First Detour: The Gap Between Talent and Leadership

One colleague, newly hired by the VP from a previous agency they'd both worked in, was promoted to Director. She was bright, capable, and deserving. I liked her and respected her work deeply. So when her promotion was questioned, the VP asked if I would help champion it—and I did. Without hesitation. Because she had earned it.

Then we hired another team member—again, someone sharp, strategic, and deeply qualified. I sat on the hiring committee, and I even raised the idea: Should she come in at a director level? I wanted what was best for the team, for the work. I wasn't bitter about their advancement. I was a part of it.

As these shifts solidified, I started to feel...invisible. Passed over. Left behind. I had done everything I was taught to do. And still, I wasn't chosen.

I decided to ask. Carefully. Casually. I sent Jane, our VP, a text:

"I know you're still shaping the team, and I don't want to rush the process. That said, I'm curious—do you see me stepping into a leadership role in the future?"

Chapter 3

Her reply was short. Final.

"Honestly, no."

That was it. No feedback. No context. No invitation to grow or even an acknowledgment of the contributions I had made. Just no.

I texted back, "Okay, thank you," and sat with it—stunned.

Later, during a 360 coaching process, I looked for clues. Feedback was vague. The most memorable line? "She's not a team player."

WTF?!

How could I not be a team player when I had championed someone else's promotion, when I had helped build the team's infrastructure, when I had shown up repeatedly to speak on behalf of the group?

That's when it hit me: the gap wasn't in performance. It was in perception.

And I wasn't going to close it with more hard work. I needed a new strategy—one that didn't involve proving myself over and over again to people who already made up their minds.

I pivoted. Quietly. I began crafting an exit strategy that would allow me to finish strong, save face, and walk out the door with my head held high and my track record intact. I didn't rage quit—I exited like a leader. Not because they saw me that way—but because I had finally started to see myself that way.

Unspoken Rules: *External Dynamics and Bias*

On paper, the agency looked diverse. Racially, ethnically—yes, the boxes were checked. It was what I call a colorized environment. But scratch beneath the surface, and you'd find something else: a deeply homogenous culture when it came to class.

There were a few of us—people who didn't come from polished pathways or Ivy pipelines. People who carried stories that didn't fit neatly into conference bios or curated career arcs. Some of them were brave enough to share those stories. They talked openly about growing up in foster care or navigating instability, and the agency held those narratives up like trophies. Look at us—we hire people with lived experience.

Chapter 3

While those stories were real and worthy, something about how they were used didn't sit right with me. It felt like personal history being turned into institutional branding. A kind of performative inclusion. I didn't want to be a poster. I wanted to be seen for my work.

So, I stayed quiet. I didn't share my background. I didn't talk about what I had overcome. To this day, I still wrestle with why.

Was I embarrassed? Maybe.

But mostly, I think I didn't want to be used. I didn't want my story to be someone else's success metric.

I remember confiding in a colleague about this—how I never felt safe enough in that space to share the truth of where I came from. I told them I didn't want to be vulnerable in a place that might weaponize my past. They said something that changed me:

"When you tell your story, no one can use it against you. It's yours. You get to decide when and how it's shared. But you have to be willing to open the door to vulnerability."

That conversation planted a seed.

It was the first time I started thinking about putting my story into writing—not as a defense, but as a decision. A way to own my narrative, rather than protect it through silence. A way to step into leadership not just through what I know but through who I am.

Because real leadership—transformational leadership—requires vulnerability.

And I was just beginning to understand what that truly meant.

What No One Tells You: *The Leadership Gap*

By the time I started to reflect on what was really happening—around me and within me—I was already well into my career. I had years of results behind me. I had the receipts. Still, I felt like I was hitting glass. Silent. Invisible. Firm.

This is what I now know as the leadership gap.

Chapter 3

> **The leadership gap** is the space between being excellent at your job and being seen as someone who can lead people, strategy, and change. It's not a reflection of your talent—it's a reflection of how your presence is perceived. And unless someone names it, unless someone teaches you to navigate it, it's easy to internalize it as failure.

For me, the gap wasn't a crack. It was a canyon.

I had mastered the technical. I was the go-to. I was the fixer, the planner, the closer. I wasn't yet seen as a leader—not because I couldn't lead, but because I hadn't made the internal **shift from doing to being**.

Here's something else no one tells you:
You can't outwork your way into leadership perception. You have to grow into it—in ways that are often invisible, emotional, and deeply personal.

The gap is especially common among high-achieving women—and especially those of us from underrepresented backgrounds. We're taught to work twice as hard, to stay ready, to master the skills. And we do. But when it's time for elevation, it's not just about what you know—it's about how others experience you. Your presence. Your confidence. Your emotional intelligence. Your ability to navigate complexity and ambiguity.

I had all the ingredients. But I hadn't yet learned how to lead with them.

And because no one told me that this was part of the process, I thought I was the problem. I thought I was doing something wrong.

I wasn't doing the wrong things—I was doing the right things at the wrong level.

It's like trying to drive a stick shift in automatic traffic. You're moving, but the engine is straining. You're out of sync with the environment you're in.

And here's the hard truth:
When you're in the gap, hard work alone won't move you forward.

You have to shift.

Not your résumé—your relationship to leadership itself.

Chapter 3

The Beginning of the Shift:
From Knowing to Becoming

Like any high achiever hitting a wall, I went straight back to what I knew best—books.

If there was a problem, I could solve it. If there was a skill I lacked, I could learn it. That was how I had always navigated life and work: study harder, know more, get better. So I threw myself into leadership reading.

I devoured books on emotional intelligence, executive presence, adaptive leadership, systems thinking, communication frameworks. I underlined sentences, made flashcards out of concepts, watched TED Talks, and listened to podcasts. I could explain the difference between technical and adaptive leadership before most people had even heard the terms. I could teach a class on humility-based leadership and strategic influence.

But I still couldn't shift how I felt in the room.

Because knowledge isn't the same as integration.

I knew what presence looked like, yet I couldn't always access it when I needed it most—when I was anxious, when I felt judged, when I was doubting myself.

I could recite feedback models and team dynamics theory, yet I struggled to find the right words when navigating conflict with peers who had more political capital.

That's when I realized: I was trying to solve an internal challenge with external tools.

I was reading about leadership—but I hadn't yet embodied it.

That's when coaching changed everything.

I came to my first executive coaching session ready to unload: complaints, confusion, disappointment. I wanted answers. A plan. A fix.

What I got were questions.

Questions that slowed me down.

Questions that turned the mirror toward me, gently, yet firmly:

- "How did you respond?"
- "What story are you telling yourself about that moment?"
- "What else might be true?"

At first, I hated it. It felt like a delay. I didn't want reflection—I wanted results.

Over time, those questions softened something in me. They made me curious again—and instead of questioning the system, I started questioning myself. They invited me to stop performing and start listening—to myself, to others, and to the energy behind the work.

Coaching taught me that leadership isn't a checklist. It's a practice, a way of being, a commitment to showing up with intention, especially when the old tools stop working.

Slowly, I began to shift. How I showed up. How I saw myself. As someone who was worthy of leadership—someone refining it, deepening it, growing into it.

A Real-Time Shift: *From Story to Strategy*

One of the most powerful questions my coach ever asked me was:

"What story are you telling yourself about that moment?"

At first, I didn't even know what that meant. I thought I was just describing facts. With her guidance—and similar insights from a trusted colleague inside the agency—I began to understand the practice:

Name the story you're telling yourself.

Then, intentionally craft an equally powerful story on the other side of the emotional spectrum. It sounded simple. In practice, it changed everything.

I remember testing this approach in a team meeting—one that, in the past, would have completely derailed me emotionally. We were reviewing proposals and deciding which external agency to partner with on a major initiative. Each of us at my level had submitted a nominee, and now we were expected to vote. On paper, it was collaborative. In

Chapter 3

reality, it felt like a popularity contest disguised as a process.

The unspoken truth was this: colleagues voted for their allies. The ones they were close to. The ones whose voices carried weight in sidebar conversations.

I didn't feel like anyone's ally.

In the past, I would have sat in silence—polite, professional, and quietly frustrated. I would have walked out of the meeting replaying every subtle slight, every vote that wasn't mine, every look I misinterpreted as judgment. I would have told myself: You're not respected. You don't belong. You're always going to be overlooked.

This time, I paused. I heard my coach's question echo in my mind:

"What story are you telling yourself?"

And then:

"What else could be true?"

I acknowledged my story: I'm not part of this inner circle. I don't have allies. This process is rigged against me.

Then I wrote a new one:

Maybe this process feels unfair to others, too. Maybe they're also navigating insecurity and uncertainty. Maybe this isn't about exclusion—it's about structure. And maybe I have more agency than I think.

That shift didn't erase the power dynamics in the room, but it freed me from being consumed by them.

Instead of shrinking or stewing, I started asking better questions:

- Why are we asked to compete in a process that's supposed to foster collaboration?
- What would it look like to co-design a system that invites alignment rather than alliance?

For the first time, I wasn't reacting—I was leading.

That's when I knew something in me had changed.

Not because the room shifted.

But because I **had**.

Once I began to shift internally, I started noticing

the other gaps in my leadership—gaps I had never been taught to value, not in a classroom, not in a training, and certainly not in a job description. The next lesson? Leadership isn't just what you know. It's who you connect with. And I had underestimated just how deeply relationships shape how you're seen.

Relational Leadership:
The Power of Being Present

As I started shedding the mindset that leadership was only about performance, another truth surfaced— one I hadn't fully grasped:

Leadership is about relationships.

Not just collaboration. Not just team dynamics. But real, human connection.

I always knew relationships mattered in theory. But I had treated them like add-ons—something you nurture when there's time, not a core part of the work itself. I thought being prepared, responsive, and excellent was enough. And in many ways, it was —until it wasn't.

This mind shift didn't come from my coach or my mentor. It came from a colleague—someone working in another part of the agency who was doing well and seemed to navigate the internal culture with ease.

One day, she casually asked me about a situation making its way through the agency. It was, in my opinion, gossip.

Proudly, I responded, "Oh, I don't know anything about that—I stay out of all the toxic stuff."

I expected her to nod in agreement. Instead, she looked...stunned.

Then she said something that completely reframed my thinking:

"That's where you get stuck. You think staying above the fray protects your integrity. But real leadership means tuning in—not to the noise, but to the dynamics underneath. The motivations. The alliances. The subtext. You don't have to participate—but you do have to understand the terrain you're leading in."

Chapter 3

She wasn't encouraging drama. She was encouraging awareness.

She explained that some of those conversations—what I dismissed as gossip—were actually how people built relationships. It's where they connected beyond the agenda. It's where trust was formed. And it's where alliances were made—so that when someone needed a voice in a room they weren't in, they had one.

She said, "Ask what someone did over the weekend. Know what their kids' names are. These things matter—not because they make you soft, but because they make you seen. And when people see you, they're more likely to stand beside you when it counts."

That was hard to hear. I prided myself on staying focused, being above the fray, keeping my head down and my work excellent. But I had confused withdrawal with integrity. And leadership requires more than being excellent—it requires being engaged.

I began to practice small shifts:

- Asking about someone's weekend.
- Noticing what brought them joy or frustration.
- Remembering a birthday or a vacation detail.

And I realized something I hadn't known I was missing: connection is strategy.

Relationships aren't just the path to influence—they're the proof that you belong.

Leadership Lesson:
Talent Gets You In the Room—But Relationships, Presence, and Perception Keep You There

For most of my career, I believed that hard work would be enough.

I was sharp, strategic, and results-driven. My technical expertise got me noticed. My performance got me promoted. I could out-strategize, out-deliver, and out-think most people in the room. So why wasn't I being seen as a leader?

Chapter 3

Because leadership isn't just about execution—it's about perception.

And perception is shaped not just by what you do, but by how you connect.

You can be exceptional at your job, and still be overlooked.

You can have the best ideas in the room, and still go unheard.

You can represent your team, advocate for others, and still be called "not a team player"—simply because the people with power don't feel connected to you.

That's the hard truth.

And the bigger truth?

Leadership is not a solo act.

It's not just what you build—it's who you build it with.

It's presence. Relationships. Trust.

It's how people feel when they experience you—not just how impressed they are by your credentials.

The First Detour: The Gap Between Talent and Leadership

What got you in the room may be talent.

What keeps you there—and elevates you beyond—is your ability to lead people, not just processes. And that requires being seen, heard, trusted, and aligned.

 **Coaching Prompt**

Who Are You Beyond the Work?

Think about the rooms you walk into—team meetings, strategic planning sessions, one-on-ones.

Before you speak, your presence is already saying something.

- What story are you telling yourself before you enter?
- Are you showing up to prove, or to connect?
- Are you being seen only for your expertise—or also for your leadership?

Now reflect on your current leadership presence:
- Do people know what matters to you outside of deadlines and deliverables?
- Have you built relationships deep enough that someone would advocate for you when you're not in the room?
- Where are you holding back, staying neutral, or staying silent—and what would it take to show up more fully?

What would shift if your leadership wasn't just defined by your competence—but also by your connection?

Call to Action: *Lead Beyond the Checklist*

It's easy to rely on technical mastery. It's familiar. It's rewarding.

But leadership doesn't live in checkboxes—it lives in the space between people.

This week, try one small shift:

- Arrive early to a meeting and ask someone how they're really doing.
- Send a note of encouragement without a task attached.
- Share one personal thing in a space where you usually stay guarded.

Don't wait for someone to give you permission to lead differently. Start now—with presence, with people, with purpose.

Because leadership isn't just what you deliver—it's how you're experienced.

Chapter 3

Want to Go Deeper?

If this chapter resonated—if you've ever felt stuck between being the go-to expert and the overlooked leader—you're not alone. And you're not without tools.

The Leadership Detour Companion Guide includes expanded journal prompts, self-coaching exercises, and real-world scenarios to help you:

- Identify where you're leading like an expert instead of like a leader
- Unpack the unspoken rules shaping perception in your workplace
- Practice relational leadership—without compromising authenticity
- Build a leadership identity rooted in connection, not just competence

You'll also explore the stories you're telling yourself—and begin to write new ones that align with your presence, not just your performance.

This companion guide is available for purchase at www.diamondconsultantsllc.com

The First Detour: The Gap Between Talent and Leadership

Turn the page.

Your leadership presence is waiting to be reclaimed.

Chapter 3

A Letter to My Earlier Leader Self

Dear Me,

You're working so hard right now.

Showing up early. Staying late. Volunteering for every extra task. Saying yes, even when you're tired. You believe, deeply, that excellence will speak for itself. That if you just keep your head down and do the work, someone will notice.

I see you.

I see the woman who leads without a title. Who carries the weight of the team on her back without complaint. Who builds the bridge and then stands guard at both ends, hoping it will earn her a seat at the table. Who thinks, maybe next time. Maybe if I just do a little more.

You're not wrong for believing in excellence. You've never needed anyone to lower the bar for you. But I need you to know this:

You are not being overlooked because you're not enough. You're being overlooked because you've been taught that being enough means staying silent, staying small, and staying out of the way.

That's not leadership. That's survival. And you've already survived enough.

I know you're hurt. I know that text—"Honestly, no"—broke something inside you.

One day, you'll realize it didn't break you.

It freed you.

It freed you from the myth that leadership is something you earn by proving yourself over and over again.

It's not.

Leadership is something you step into when you stop waiting to be chosen—and choose yourself instead.

You will learn that connection is just as powerful as competence.

That your presence matters as much as your performance.

That you don't need to shrink, code-switch, or overextend to be seen as a leader.

You already are one. You just haven't fully believed it yet.

Chapter 3

So take a breath.

Keep showing up.

But stop editing your brilliance. Stop filtering your fire.

Because the rooms that don't see you?

They don't deserve to shape your reflection.

And the leader you're becoming?

She's already proud of you.

With love,

Your Future Self

Part II:
Navigating the Detours

Chapter 4
Hitting a Wall:
When Hard Work Isn't Enough

The moment I hit the wall didn't come after a failure —it came at what I thought was the height of my career. I had just landed what felt like a dream role, appointed to lead a flagship project at a national organization. The kind of opportunity I had worked my whole life for. The kind of role that, on paper, signified arrival.

I was ready—confident, accomplished, and proud to bring both my lived experience and my expertise into a space that had rarely welcomed voices like mine.

But the wall hit fast. And it hit hard.

When Voice Becomes a Weapon— *Even Against Yourself*

As impressive as I may have looked, I carried quiet

insecurities that hadn't fully surfaced—until this role. Chief among them was my voice.

I'm from the South, and I carry a distinct Southern drawl—something I once tried to hide, then tried to neutralize, and eventually tried to make peace with. But in corporate and executive settings, I often felt like my voice worked against me. I feared it made me sound "less than," even when my content was sharp and my credentials unshakable.

That fear was confirmed—at least in my mind—during a supervision meeting with the fourth supervisor I had in my first three years in the role. The first person who hired me resigned before I even started. The second and third leaders were interim or short-term. But this one, a white woman with a soft, almost whispery tone, pulled me aside and said, "Sometimes I have trouble understanding you... it's your accent."

The words landed like a punch.

What made it worse was that we had recently welcomed a new team member—also from the

Chapter 4

South. A white woman with a much stronger accent than mine. I'd overheard colleagues compliment her Southern charm more than once. Her drawl was endearing. Mine, apparently, needed correction.

That moment unsettled something in me.

As part of my professional development, I enrolled in a diction and speaking course. I told the coach I wanted to "fix" my voice. I expected technical drills. I expected to be told what to drop or shift. But after a few assessments, the speech coach looked at me and said, "You're one of the most well-spoken professionals I've worked with. Your voice? It's not the problem. Your accent? It's beautiful. What we all have—are accents."

Instead, we worked on small mechanics—like my lifelong struggle to say "point" correctly (I always said "purnt," thanks to what I now know are diphthongs).

Still, that supervisor's comment lingered. I began second-guessing myself in meetings. Watching my words. Pausing before I spoke. I was back to editing myself before others could do it for me. And even though I'd always been praised for my public speaking, for a while, I doubted it all.

What I know now is that the leadership wall doesn't just appear in our environment—it builds inside us too. It's constructed from every moment we begin to question whether we truly belong.

On my first day in the office, I met with the colleague who would co-lead the initiative with me. I was eager to collaborate, to get to work. But within minutes, she suggested how we might divide responsibilities: "You can lead the community portion, and I'll lead the systems change work."

I didn't say much at that moment, but inside, I was unsettled. I couldn't fully explain it— I just knew I was offended. Viscerally.

Was it the assumption that I couldn't do systems work?

Was it the subtle framing of me as "the community person"—the insider, the recipient—not as a strategist or equal?

Was it the shame that I was being positioned as

someone to be represented by systems, rather than someone capable of reimagining and changing them?

In retrospect, it was all of those things. And that moment—those first few minutes of my first day—marked the high point of our relationship.

From there, things only deteriorated.

The Power Struggle Behind the Politeness

Up until my appointment, my co-lead had been seen as the face of the flagship program. She led the early design and was the point of contact for many of the systems and city partners. When I came in as her equal—a peer—the dynamic shifted. It didn't sit easily. Not with her. Not with the room.

Within my first week, a major site visit was scheduled with one of the program's anchor partners. I was excited. I had spent days immersing myself in the work, learning the background, reviewing notes, asking questions. I didn't expect to lead on day one—but I did expect to be present. I wanted to listen, learn, observe the dynamics, and begin building relationships. I handled all the travel logistics, ready to show up with intention.

Then I got the email.

She wrote that she had spoken with the site lead, and they felt that my presence might be "disruptive." She said it as if she were doing me a favor—giving me a heads-up, relaying their concern. But her language was sharp: "They want to ask that you not attend."

I read it three times. My heart sank. The word "disruptive" echoed louder each time.

What was it about me that would be disruptive? They hadn't met me. Hadn't spoken to me. I hadn't even been introduced. I was the new co-lead, and I had been excluded from a conversation that directly impacted my role.

I went home that night in tears. It was my first week. I should've been building excitement and momentum. Instead, I was left questioning my place and fighting back shame. Her actions weren't just undermining—they were crushing.

Chapter 4

I called the person who oversaw the initiative. I explained what happened, and thankfully, they were clear: "This is your decision to make. We hired you as co-lead. We trust your judgment. Weigh the pros and cons—and do what you believe is right."

I did.

I went.

The site visit started with tension in the air. I could sense the hesitation, the side glances, the unspoken curiosity about why I had shown up. But I showed up with clarity, not combativeness. I listened. I asked questions. I demonstrated that I wasn't there to take over—I was there to contribute. By the end of the day, I had built a rapport with several team members and laid a foundation for mutual respect.

I never asked my co-lead why she used the word disruptive. I didn't confront her about the way that call had gone down behind closed doors. I didn't need to. The damage was done. That one move—made under the guise of "team communication"—set the tone for everything that followed.

From the moment I arrived, I was in a quiet power struggle. One that was never named, never addressed, yet always felt. The tension wasn't about the work—it was about territory, about who got to lead, who got to be visible, and who got to belong.

After the site visit, something in me shifted. While I had shown up, stood my ground, and earned respect–the damage to the working relationship was done. I no longer felt like a collaborator. I felt like a contender–someone who had to prove her value in a space that had quietly questioned her right to be there from the start.

I did what many of us do when we're put under an unspoken microscope. I started to overcompensate.

I worked harder. Showed up smarter. Came over prepared to every meeting. I smiled even when I was unraveling inside. I observed and mirrored how others dressed. I shifted my tone. I carefully controlled my body language. I made sure I never showed frustration—even though I was filled with it.

Chapter 4

Smiles, Flowers, and Invisible Walls

When I arrived on my first day, there was a beautiful welcome waiting for me—a large basket and an elegant bouquet of flowers from the Office of the President. A card signed by the then president. It was thoughtful. It was symbolic. It said: "I see you. I'm glad you're here."

But symbolism and sincerity are not always the same thing.

That same morning, I handed the administrative professional a short list of office supplies I needed to get started—standard items: pens, pads, markers, sticky notes, a whiteboard. I said thank you and headed to lunch, feeling hopeful, energized, and ready to dig in. When I returned, the items weren't there.

Instead, sitting on my desk was an office supply catalog and a post-it with a number to call.

Her message was clear: Get it yourself.

At first, I brushed it off. Maybe it was a miscommunication. Maybe she was too busy. Weeks later, I found out—through casual conversation—that she had regularly ordered supplies for other team members, including another Black woman in the office. It wasn't that she didn't place orders. It was that she didn't place them for me.

That moment scratched a truth I hadn't faced. It exposed her. More importantly, it exposed the ecosystem I had entered. A small action. A loud message: Don't get too comfortable. Know your place.

It was a different kind of wall than I was used to, not the overt kind, not the shouted kind. This was the kind built from micro-boundaries and professional politeness. One where everyone smiled—and yet, you could still feel the power dynamics pressing against your confidence.

And just like the times before, I tried to silence my insecurity with performance. I doubled down. I worked harder, showed up earlier, stayed later. I said yes when I wanted to say maybe. Said thank you when I wanted to ask why.

Chapter 4

When you're one of the first—or one of the only—there's an unspoken pressure not just to succeed, but to prove that your presence is justified. That you're not a favor. That you're not a risk.

I didn't want to be the problem. I didn't want to cause a stir. I wanted to earn my place.

Looking back, I see that I was trying to earn something I had already been given—**and that's the trap**. The moment you start proving your worth instead of standing in it, you begin negotiating your identity just to survive.

The Questions That Changed Everything

In the midst of all this, I started having regular conversations with a colleague I respected—someone who had observed my work and recognized my struggle, even if I wasn't fully naming it myself. He didn't offer advice. He didn't try to "fix" anything. What he did offer were questions.

I didn't want questions—I wanted answers. I wanted to know what I was doing wrong, how to fix it, how to win them over, how to succeed in a place that

that didn't seem to want me. Still, the questions stuck with me. I'd go home and think about the answer and about why the question was being asked in the first place.

That's when I was offered an executive coach.

I thought, perfect. Now I'll get a strategy, a game plan. Instead, the questions continued.

I remember telling my coach how I didn't respond to things that were said in meetings—even when they were clearly offensive—because I wanted to remain professional. That was how I had been taught to show up: poised, composed, in control.

She paused, then asked: "What's your definition of professional?"

It stopped me. Cold.

We spent two sessions unpacking that question. Where did my definition of professionalism come from? What did it mean to me? Who taught it to me—and who was I trying to protect by holding onto it so tightly?

Then she asked another question: "When you don't

Chapter 4

respond to someone who's said something inappropriate or offensive, how do you think that silence might be interpreted?"

It had never occurred to me that my silence might not be seen as grace or professionalism—but as coldness. Or worse, indifference.

Suddenly, I began to realize something I had never questioned before: In my effort to be "professional," I was denying myself honesty. I was holding everything in, until it spilled out in ways that felt out of proportion. I thought I was managing my emotions—when in truth, I was suppressing them. And that suppression was damaging both me and my relationships.

Then my coach introduced me to a new word: **Calibrate.**

"Responding and reacting," she said, "are not the same thing. Your job isn't to suppress—it's to calibrate, to learn how to be honest and strategic, to show up with presence, not performance."

That word—calibrate—changed everything for me. For the first time, I understood there was a middle ground. I didn't have to choose between silence and explosion. I could choose truth with intention.

I began to understand something else, too: That the root of my struggle wasn't competence. It wasn't even credibility. It was connection.

I wasn't building relationships. I wasn't letting people see me. I wasn't allowing space for trust.
And for a leader, that's everything.

You don't have to abandon your composure to stand in your truth. You can calibrate. You can choose presence over performance.

 **Coaching Prompt**

Reclaiming Your Voice

We all carry stories about our voices—how they sound, how they're received, and what they signal to others.

- Have you ever been made to feel that your voice was too much—too loud, too soft, too different, too Southern, too

emotional, too direct?
- Have you ever tried to shrink or smooth out your voice to make others more comfortable?
- What part of your voice have you hidden—not just how you speak, but how you express your truth?
- And what would it look like to reclaim it—not to prove anything, but simply because your voice belongs?

Your voice is not a flaw to fix. It is an instrument of power, identity, and presence. The goal isn't to erase it—it's to own it.

The System Wasn't Broken—It Was Working As Designed

At some point during that season, I stopped blaming myself. Not immediately, but slowly, steadily, I began to see the patterns—in my experience and in the architecture of the environment around me.

I wasn't failing. I was swimming upstream in a

current designed for someone else.

The systems I was working within weren't neutral. They were built on unspoken norms about who gets to lead, who gets to speak, and who gets to belong. These weren't rules written in policy manuals—they were embedded in culture, in tone, in expectations. They often operated under the guise of professionalism, collaboration, and fit.

It wasn't until I was introduced to *The Practice of Adaptive Leadership* that something clicked into place. Early in the book, the authors state:

"There is no such thing as a dysfunctional organization, because every organization is perfectly aligned to achieve the results it currently gets."

That one line illuminated everything. While I had been describing the organization as dysfunctional, what I came to realize was that it was functioning exactly as its leadership—whether consciously or not—was allowing it to function. In other words, the system wasn't broken. It was working. Just not for me.

Chapter 4

When organizations say they want diversity, but quietly reward assimilation...

When they highlight inclusion, but never interrogate power...

When they celebrate your hiring, but never support your presence...

That's not an oversight. That's a system functioning by design.

I used to internalize the tension I felt—believing I was too sensitive, too eager, too uncertain. But I've since learned that many leaders, especially Black women, carry the weight of trying to lead in systems that were never truly meant to hold us. We are not just navigating jobs—we are navigating legacies of exclusion, codes of conduct never written with our realities in mind.

In spaces like that, excellence isn't always enough. In fact, it can be threatening. Your confidence may be mistaken for arrogance, your questions interpreted as resistance, your cultural expressions labeled as unprofessional.

That's the part no one warns you about.

The real work of leadership, I've learned, isn't just about strategy or execution. It's about navigating **systems** while holding onto **self**.

Sometimes, it's about disrupting the systems from within—without letting it erase you in the process.

There's nothing wrong with structure. But structure without awareness becomes rigidity. And rigidity without reflection becomes harm.

We talk so much about imposter syndrome, but rarely do we talk about **imposter systems**—ones that demand you prove your worth twice and still question it after you've delivered. Systems that ask for your brilliance yet flinch when it shines too brightly.

That season taught me that part of becoming a powerful leader isn't just managing the politics of the role—it's learning to see the structure for what it is. And deciding, with clarity and courage, how you will lead anyway.

Chapter 4

Before I Had the Words

Years before this role—before the platform, the pressure, and the polish—I lived and worked in St. Thomas. It was one of the most formative seasons of my career. The budget was modest. The resources were limited. But the connections? The clarity? The confidence? It was unmatched.

My voice was heard. My ideas mattered. There were no politics around who got to speak first or whose presence needed to be managed. I didn't have to calibrate or code-switch or decode how to show up. I just…showed up.

One afternoon, I led a planning meeting with local partners about expanding services for youth and families. We sat in a room with fans spinning above us and the Caribbean breeze slipping through open windows. There were no flashy slide decks. Just a whiteboard, a marker, and my full presence.

I spoke with ease—Southern roots mingling with island rhythm. I shared a vision for the work grounded in listening, dignity, and partnership. People leaned in.

After the meeting, a partner pulled me aside and said, "I don't know what it is, but when you speak, it lands." That line stayed with me— because it reminded me that being myself had power. That truth didn't need translation to be respected.

I often look back at that version of myself—not with nostalgia, but with reverence. She didn't have the title. She didn't have the corner office. She had her voice. She had her values. She led without permission—and people followed.

I think of her now when I coach others—especially those who feel stuck, silenced, or invisible in their current roles. Because sometimes we forget who we were before the edits. We forget what it felt like to be fully received, to speak without rehearsal, to trust our knowing without needing three credentials and five validations.

That younger version of me didn't have the language for systems thinking. She didn't yet know about power dynamics, adaptive leadership, or emotional intelligence. But she knew something sacred about speaking your truth—and she wasn't afraid to do it.

Chapter 4

Somewhere along the way, I started trading that sacred truth for structure. And this chapter of my life—this wall I hit—wasn't just a breakdown. It was a call to return.

 **Reflection**

Remembering Who You Were Before the Edits

Take a moment to reconnect with a version of yourself that felt most whole—before the expectations, before the performance, before the edits.

- Where were you?
- What work were you doing?
- How did you speak, move, lead?
- Who were you when you didn't feel the need to rehearse or shrink?

Now ask yourself:

- What did that version of you know that you've since forgotten?
- What part of that you do you miss?
- What would it look like to bring her back

into your leadership today—not in rebellion, but in restoration?

You don't have to go back in time to reconnect with that power.

You carry her still.

Let her speak.

Leadership Lesson:
Recognizing Leadership Plateaus

Leadership plateaus don't arrive with flashing lights. They show up in subtler ways—through tension, burnout, frustration, or that quiet voice whispering, "I've done everything right...so why do I feel stuck?"

It's a disorienting space. On paper, you're accomplished. You've hit milestones. Maybe even the one you thought was the dream. Yet, something feels off. The momentum that once carried you begins to fade. The things that used to work—working hard, staying ready, staying late—don't create the same results. The praise thins out. The clarity blurs. The confidence wavers.

Chapter 4

This is the moment when titles, talent, and task-completion hit their ceiling. It's the moment when leadership stops being about performance—and starts being about presence.

If no one ever told you that leadership requires more than skill...

That it demands relationship, emotional self-awareness, and the courage to be seen...

Then of course you double down on what's always worked: perfection, production, and proving your worth.

Here's the truth: a plateau isn't failure.

It's feedback.

It's not a stop sign. It's a mirror.

It's the moment life says: "You've grown as far as you can on this version of you. Now it's time to evolve."

The most dangerous part of a leadership plateau isn't being stuck.

It's pretending that you're not.

When you ignore the signs—when you silence the

discomfort—you delay the growth that discomfort is trying to spark.

In my coaching work, I see this all the time: brilliant, high-performing leaders who feel like they're losing their edge. It's not because they've stopped being good—it's because the metrics of "good" have changed. The room is asking more of them, not for more output, but for more self. More wisdom. More clarity. More courage.

That's the shift.

At some point in every leader's journey, you're no longer evaluated by how much you produce. You are measured by how deeply you lead, by how well you know yourself, how effectively you influence others, by how authentically you show up.

Leadership isn't just the next step in your career. It's the next evolution of your identity.

You cannot evolve by staying who you were.

You cannot grow by hiding what makes you powerful.

And you cannot lead powerfully while shrinking

silently.

Plateaus invite us to pause, not to stop, to recalibrate, not to retreat.

They ask: Who do you need to become in order to move forward?

The answer is almost never "more of what you've already been."

The answer is usually: More of who you already are, unedited.

> "Your plateau isn't a punishment. It's a portal. The next version of your leadership is waiting on the next version of you."
> —Dr. Tammi Fleming

Call to Action:
Naming Your Leadership Plateau

If you've ever found yourself thinking, "I've done everything right... so why do I feel stuck?"—you're not alone.

Leadership plateaus are quiet. They don't always show up as failure. Sometimes, they show up as silence, as a lack of opportunity, as an invisible barrier you can't quite name—but feel every day.

They don't always feel like a crisis. Sometimes they feel like boredom, like burnout, like overachievement with no reward, like constantly adjusting who you are to stay in a room that isn't adjusting to meet you.

But you can't move through what you won't name.

The first step toward breakthrough is recognition—not blame, not fixing, just truth.

Guided Exercise

Take a moment. Write freely. Name your wall.

1 Ask yourself:

- Where in your leadership do you feel like the needle's not moving?
- What strategies have stopped working—but you keep using them anyway?

Chapter 4

- What unspoken rules are you still following, even though they're costing you parts of yourself?
- What version of you has plateaued? And what version is trying to emerge?

② Now, open your journal, a blank document, or even your phone's notes app.

Take 10–15 minutes and complete this sentence:

If I'm honest, the real reason I feel stuck right now is…

No edits. No audience. No filter.

Just honesty.

Because honesty is the seed of every transformation. And your leadership will only evolve to the level of truth you're willing to stand in.

This isn't about fixing yourself.

This is about finding yourself again—beneath the performance, the pressure, and the perfection.

Your plateau isn't a dead end. It's a turning point.

Choose the turn.

Want to Go Deeper?

This chapter was designed to help you name the wall.

But the real work happens when you start climbing —or dismantling—it.

In **The Leadership Detour Companion Guide**, you'll find:

- A guided journaling exercise to map out your leadership plateau
- A framework to identify the beliefs, behaviors, and boundaries keeping you stuck
- A personal audit tool to help you shift from performance to presence
- Reflection questions to help you redefine what "professional" means for you

This companion guide is available for purchase at
www.diamondconsultantsllc.com

Your next level of leadership is waiting on your next level of truth.

Chapter 5
The Breakthrough

"Breakthrough doesn't happen when the world changes. It happens when you do."

—Dr. Tammi Fleming

Coaching Changed Everything

It wasn't immediate. Coaching didn't fix my environment. It didn't make the microaggressions stop or instantly grant me the power to navigate difficult conversations with grace. But it changed me. Once I started shifting internally, everything else began to follow.

The truth is, I didn't come into coaching with full buy-in. At first, I treated it like any other professional development opportunity—something to study, master, and move on from. I thought: Let me just get a few strategies, a framework or two, and I'll be fine. I didn't realize coaching wasn't about learning something new—it was about unlearning the ways I had been trained to lead, especially under pressure.

In one of our early sessions, I remember my coach asking me how I was really doing. Not in the "polite workplace" way. But in a way that expected an honest answer. I paused. I defaulted to: "You know, it's challenging... I'm managing." She didn't let it go. She asked again. "How are you doing?"

That's when it cracked.

I blurted out, "I feel attacked. There's an undercurrent in how they show up, and I feel like I'm drowning in it." It was the first time I'd said it out loud—not just to someone else, but to myself.

She didn't try to reframe it right away. She didn't tell me to stay positive or focus on what I could control. She sat with it. With me. Then she asked something that stopped me in my tracks:

"What are your options when you're in an unhealthy environment—but not ready to leave?"

That question unnerved me.

Because the truth was—I didn't want to leave. Not

Chapter 5

yet. I had moved my entire life for this opportunity. Leaving would've felt like failure. Like letting others win. Like breaking a promise to myself. But staying without a strategy was just slow erosion.

What I hadn't realized was that I'd been trying to survive the situation using the same tools that got me there: performance, perfectionism, over-preparedness. Those tools weren't working anymore.

Coaching gave me permission to put those tools down. The tools weren't wrong. They were incomplete.

Instead of asking me to push harder, my coach asked me to go deeper.

We began naming fears. External and internal fears. She asked me to list the people or behaviors that triggered my fear response. Then she said, "What would it look like to face each one with calibration?"

Not confrontation.

Not collapse.

Calibration.

It was a new language, a new muscle, and the

beginning of a breakthrough.

Practicing in Real Life

The first time I tried to calibrate in a real setting, I felt like my entire body was on high alert. My palms were sweaty. My heart raced. My voice—normally steady—shook just enough for me to hear it. I did it anyway.

There had been a pattern with one of my colleagues. In meetings, they would often interrupt me mid-sentence or repeat my points using different language—language that somehow landed better with the room. It was subtle. It was consistent. And it was starting to chip away at my confidence.

Before coaching, I would have swallowed the frustration. Told myself I was imagining it. Maybe I didn't make the point clearly enough. Maybe I needed to sharpen my delivery. I would've gone into overdrive to fix something that wasn't mine to fix.

This time, I didn't shrink. I chose calibration.

After a team meeting, I asked the colleague if they

Chapter 5

had a few minutes. I didn't rehearse a long script. I didn't lace it with sugar to make it easier to hear. I just took a deep breath and said:

"I want to bring something to your attention that's been sitting with me. In our meetings, I've noticed a pattern where I'll raise a point, and it's often repeated later in different language. I know it may not be intentional. However, the impact is that my contributions feel invisible. And I wanted to name it because I value working with you—and I'd like us to reset that dynamic."

Then I waited.

The silence felt like hours. It was probably just five seconds. They looked surprised—maybe even a little defensive. Then a slow nod and a reply, "I hadn't realized that. I appreciate you telling me."

That was it. Not a full transformation. Not a dramatic apology. Just acknowledgement. And the next time we were in a meeting together, they made a point to say, "I want to build on Tammi's idea..."

It seems small. But in that moment, it felt huge.

The breakthrough wasn't just in how they responded—it was in how I showed up.

I didn't fold. I didn't perform. I didn't explode. I calibrated. That changed everything.

The Power of a Dual Support System

Coaching gave me the structure, accountability, and deep self-reflection I needed. But in the beginning—when I was learning how to stretch muscles I'd never used before—it wasn't always enough on its own.

My coach was incredible. She held space for me to unpack years of habits, explore new language, and role-play tough conversations. We met biweekly, and each session was packed with insight. But coaching required scheduling. It was intentional, strategic, and bound by time.

I also needed someone I could call in the in-between moments—the moments where self-doubt crept in, where I second-guessed whether I should speak up, where I needed a gut check before trying something new.

Chapter 5

That's where my informal mentor came in.

She was a trusted colleague –someone who had walked with me through seasons of growth, someone who knew my leadership style, my values, and my heart. She didn't need me to be polished. She just needed me to be honest. She always met that honesty with care and clarity.

One of the most pivotal conversations I had during that time didn't happen in a coaching session or a team meeting. It happened in my car—engine off, phone in hand, sitting outside the office trying to pull myself together after a hard week.

I had just left a leadership meeting where, once again, I felt sidelined. I had raised a concern about a program rollout, backed it up with data, and offered a strategic alternative. The conversation moved on without acknowledgement. Ten minutes later, another colleague raised the same concern—almost word for word—and suddenly the room engaged.

Nods. Questions. Validation.

By the end of the meeting, I was spiraling internally:

Why did my words fall flat? Am I invisible here? Am I overreacting?

I texted my mentor four words: "Do you have time?"

She called almost immediately. No small talk. Just, "What's up?"

I told her everything. She didn't interrupt. She didn't downplay it. She listened with the kind of quiet that says, I believe you. Then she asked, "What did you want to do in that moment—but didn't?"

I said, "I wanted to name it, out loud, but I froze. I didn't want to seem angry. I didn't want to be the one who 'makes it about race' or 'makes it about gender.' I just wanted to be heard without having to perform."

She paused. Then said, "Okay. Let's back up. What exactly did you want to say? Say it to me like I'm in that room."

I took a breath—and then I did. She gave me notes—not to sanitize it, but to help me anchor it in clarity and impact. Then she said something I'll never forget:

"You don't have to pick between being graceful and

being direct. You just need to be clear—and be you. Don't wait until you're boiling over. Say it while you still have your voice."

That conversation grounded me. It didn't just affirm what I felt—it gave me a strategy. She didn't tell me to quit or "rise above it." She helped me reclaim my voice before it cracked.

In the weeks that followed, I kept her words close. Whenever I found myself shrinking in a meeting or second-guessing whether to speak up, I'd hear her: "Say it while you still have your voice."

That's the power of mentorship in real time.
It doesn't always come with a schedule or structure—it comes with presence, with truth, with care.

Two Lanes of Growth: *Coaching vs. Mentoring*

Coaching and mentoring supported me in different ways—both were essential. If I had to describe them in motion, I'd say:

- Coaching moved me inward and forward.
- Mentoring kept me grounded in who I was

and what I was learning in real-time.

Coaching was where I went to excavate patterns, ask hard questions, and reframe my thinking. It was structured, sacred, and often uncomfortable—in the best way. My coach didn't give me answers. She held up a mirror and helped me look deeper. She challenged my assumptions. She pushed me to recalibrate instead of react. And most importantly, she helped me lead myself through the fog.

Mentoring, on the other hand, was more fluid. It met me where I was. It was the text before the meeting, the call in the car, the "gut check" after an unexpected encounter. My mentor didn't just understand leadership—she understood my leadership. She helped me translate the insights from coaching into daily practice. She reminded me of who I was when I was tempted to forget. And sometimes, she just said, "You're not wrong—and you're not alone."

Chapter 5

Here's how I now think of the difference:

COACHING	MENTORING
Focuses on *growth* and *transformation*	**Focuses** on *guidance* and *real-world navigation*
Asks questions to *spark reflection*	**Shares** *insight* and *experience*
Builds *self-awareness* and *leadership identity*	**Offers** real-time *wisdom* and *support*
Encourages you to *find your own answers*	**Helps** you *avoid landmines* based on lived experience
Often **formal**, *time-bound*	Often **informal**, *relational*

Table 1: Comparing Coaching and Mentoring

Having both changed everything. One helped me discover who I was becoming. The other helped me survive who I was becoming.

I've come to believe that every leader needs at least one of each:

- Someone who will ask: "What's the story you're telling yourself?"

- And someone who will say: "You're doing better than you think."

The combination gave me the confidence to understand the true meaning of leadership—and to embody it with clarity, care, and courage.

Leadership Lesson: *The Power of Being Open*

There's a myth that strong leaders have it all figured out. That they always speak with certainty. That they always know the next move. That vulnerability is optional—and openness is weakness.

However, the most transformative moments in my leadership journey didn't come when I was polished. They came when I was open.

Open doesn't mean unprepared. It doesn't mean falling apart or handing over your power.

Being open is a strategic posture.

It's the willingness to see things clearly—even when what you see challenges your ego.

When I started working with a coach, I thought I just needed a new toolkit. What I didn't realize was that

Chapter 5

my biggest breakthrough wouldn't come from technique—it would come from truth. And truth only arrives when you invite it in.

That invitation requires openness.

Openness to hard questions.

Openness to new languages.

Openness to the idea that some of what I was experiencing wasn't just about the environment—it was about the internal stories I'd been telling myself for years.

Here's what I learned:
- Openness creates awareness. It helps you recognize the difference between what's happening and what you're projecting.
- Openness brings clarity. It peels back the layers of habit, fear, and assumption to show what's really there.
- Openness fuels growth. It's the ground where change takes root—because you can't transform what you're not willing to examine.

And openness takes strength. **It takes far more strength to pause, reflect, and receive than it does**

to power through.

My mentor said it best:

"Everyone doesn't have the mindset to grow. The difference is—you were open."

That didn't mean I was fearless. I was scared half the time. But I was open to growth. I didn't just want to look strong—I wanted to be strong. Strong enough to admit what wasn't working. Strong enough to let someone help me reframe it. Strong enough to let go of outdated definitions of professionalism and power.

That openness? It didn't weaken me. It anchored me. It sharpened my instincts. It quieted my defensiveness. It helped me lead with more presence and less performance.

If you're in a season where you feel stuck or disoriented, don't just ask, "What's wrong?"
Ask, "What am I resisting?"

Sometimes the barrier isn't the situation.

It's your unwillingness to see it differently.

Chapter 5

Once you become open to the possibility that the shift starts with you—clarity will start to flow.

Not all at once, just enough to take the next step, and then the next.

Fixed Mindset vs. Growth Mindset: *Why Openness Matters*

What I was learning through coaching—and living through in practice—was what psychologist Carol Dweck calls a **growth mindset**. It's the belief that skills, intelligence, and leadership capacity aren't fixed traits. They can be developed. Strengthened. Expanded.

Most of us are raised—and praised—within a **fixed mindset** system:

- Be the smartest.
- Don't make mistakes.
- Stay in control.
- Prove you know what you're doing.

We learn to perform, to perfect, to protect our image at all costs.

Here's the danger of a fixed mindset in leadership: it turns every challenge into a threat.

If you're not open, you can't learn.

If you can't learn, you can't grow.

If you can't grow, your leadership plateaus—even if your résumé keeps expanding.

Openness is the foundation of a **growth mindset**—and growth mindset is the foundation of powerful leadership.

Leaders with a fixed mindset focus on looking competent. Leaders with a growth mindset focus on **becoming** more capable.

That distinction changed everything for me.
I stopped needing to have all the answers.
I started learning how to ask better questions.
I gave myself permission to evolve—not just externally, but internally.

That's the real work of breakthrough leadership.

Not changing your title.

Changing your **thinking**.

Chapter 5

Reflection

Is Your Mindset Helping You Lead—or Just Helping You Cope?

Take a moment to reflect on how you show up when things get uncomfortable in your leadership. Be honest—not to judge yourself, but to know yourself.

Ask yourself:

- When was the last time I avoided feedback because I didn't want to feel exposed?
- Where in my leadership do I focus more on looking competent than becoming capable?
- What challenge have I labeled as "personal" that might actually be an opportunity for growth?
- Where am I clinging to control instead of staying curious?

Journal Starter: *If I'm honest, the mindset I've been leading from lately is…*

Now finish this sentence: *If I chose to lead with a growth mindset, I would…*

No edits. No filters. Just truth.
That's where the shift begins.

Build Your Leadership Support Circle

Leadership can be lonely. Especially when you're evolving.

You may be outgrowing relationships that once grounded you, questioning systems that once affirmed you, or shedding versions of yourself that no longer serve you. It's sacred work. And sacred doesn't mean solitary. You're not meant to carry it alone.

Behind every breakthrough is a conversation, a truth-teller, a guide, or a moment of reflection that sparked a shift. That's why one of the most powerful things you can do as a leader is to **intentionally build your Leadership Support Circle**—a personal group of trusted people who can help you grow with courage and clarity.

Think of it like a personal board of directors—not for

your business, but for your becoming.

These are the people who:
- Tell you the truth, even when it's hard
- Ask the questions that push your thinking forward
- See your potential and hold you accountable
- Offer perspective when your vision gets cloudy
- Remind you who you are when you forget

But let's be honest: not everyone is equipped to hold that space.

It's tempting to fill your circle with the people who love you most—your best friend, your biggest cheerleader, the colleague who always validates you. While those people matter deeply, they may not always be able to offer what your growth requires.

Growth doesn't just need support.

It needs **structure**.

It needs **strategy**.

It needs **someone who will say**:

"I love you—but here's what I see."

"You're not wrong—but you're not off the hook."

> "This version of you was necessary—but so is the next one."

That kind of honesty is rare. It's not always easy to hear. But it's where transformation begins.

Roles for Your Leadership Support Circle

You don't need a large group. You need the right group. Think of it in three roles:

ROLE	DESCRIPTION	EXAMPLE QUESTIONS
The Mirror	Reflects your patterns, behaviors, and blind spots with care and clarity	*"What are you avoiding right now?"*
The Key	Opens doors to new thinking, challenges assumptions, and helps reframe	*"What would shift if you saw this differently?"*
The Anchor	Grounds you emotionally and reminds you of your values when you feel shaky	*"What do you know to be true about yourself right now?"*

Table 2: Roles for Your Leadership Support Circle

Chapter 5

You may find one person who holds all three roles. Or you may have different people for each. What matters is intention. Choose people who support your growth, not just your grind.

 **Guided Exercise**

Take Inventory of the People in Your Circle

① **Ask yourself:**
- Who do I call when I need a reality check—not just reassurance?
- Who tells me the truth, not just what I want to hear?
- Who helps me think clearly, not just vent emotionally?
- Who challenges me to be better, even when it's uncomfortable?

And then ask the hard one:
- Who am I keeping close out of habit, comfort, or fear of being alone?

② **Record Your Response:**
- *If I built my Leadership Support Circle based on*

who grows me—not just who knows me—it would include...

③ Create It:
- Identify 2–3 people who fit the roles above.
- Reach out—set an intention for the relationship. It doesn't have to be formal. Just clear.
- Check in quarterly. Ask: "What's shifted in my leadership? What do I need now?"

Closing Thought

The truth is: **You are not the problem.**
However, you might be standing in your own way.
The good news?
You don't have to move through it alone.
You just have to choose who you'll let walk beside you.

> *"You don't have to perform to be powerful. You don't have to pretend to be prepared. You're allowed to grow out loud. That's what real leadership looks like."*
> —Dr. Tammi Fleming

Chapter 5

> **Want to Go Deeper?**
>
> The breakthrough starts with awareness.
>
> But it's the integration that sustains your growth.
>
> In **The Leadership Detour Companion Guide: Chapter 5 Companion**, you'll explore:
>
> - A reflection exercise to assess your current support system
> - A worksheet to design your Leadership Support Circle
> - Journal prompts to clarify where you need support—and where you may be resisting it
> - A leadership mindset tracker to help shift from reaction to calibration
>
> Download your digital or print copy at
> **www.diamondconsultantsllc.com**

Turn the page.
The next version of your leadership is waiting—and it's not just more skilled. It's more supported, more self-aware, and more aligned.

Chapter 6
Mastering Emotional Intelligence

She came into our first coaching session confident and self-aware—or so I thought.

"I'm actually really proud of my emotional intelligence," she said, smiling. "It's something I've worked on a lot."

I believed her. She was composed, articulate, and technically brilliant. A Ph.D. with deep expertise in her field, she was the kind of leader people turned to for answers. As she began to share the story of a recent meeting, something told me there was more beneath the surface.

She was describing a tense exchange with another executive—specifically, another executive woman from a partner organization. The meeting had been her idea. She'd called it to bring clarity to a project that had started to unravel. But from the moment it began, she said, she felt ambushed.

"She just started in on me," she said, eyes narrowing

Chapter 6

slightly. "Like, question after question—rapid fire. I couldn't even respond. I just sat there and let her finish. Then I said, 'Wait a minute. I asked for this meeting.'"

She went on to explain that she calmly laid out her reasoning for calling the meeting. She clarified key points, pointed out where her colleague had bypassed proper channels, and tried to keep the conversation productive. "I never raised my voice," she told me, "and I was really aware of my response —or, I guess, my non-response."

I listened. But I also noticed something else— something familiar. She was telling me a version of the story I used to tell myself. One where being "calm" and "professional" was a badge of emotional intelligence. Where not reacting was the same as managing your emotions. And I could hear, just under her words, the echo of something unprocessed.

I asked her to start again.

This time, I interrupted early.

"When she started firing those questions," I said, "what were you thinking?"

She blinked, surprised. "I was livid," she said. "I was thinking, 'Wait, I asked for this meeting. Why is she interrogating me?'"

"And what were you feeling?"

She hesitated. "My heart was racing. I could feel it in my chest. I was trying really hard to control it."

"So, why didn't you stop her?"

She looked down. "Because I didn't want her to think I was flustered."

We sat with that.

Then I asked, "When you didn't respond and held your emotions in—what do you think she thought?"

Her first answer was immediate: "That I was professional. That I handled it well."

I nodded. "That's one story," I said. "Now tell me another. What's an equally possible interpretation of your silence?"

She looked confused. "What do you mean?"

Chapter 6

"There are always three stories in a moment like this," I explained. "The story we tell ourselves, the story the other person might tell, and the possible truth somewhere in between."

She sat with that. For a long moment, she said nothing.

Then: "Maybe she thought I didn't understand what she was saying. Or that I was ignoring her. Or... maybe she thought I didn't care."

We kept pulling on that thread. I asked her to reflect on her reaction. Then on the other woman's. Why might she have come into the meeting so aggressively? What insecurities might have been driving her behavior? What assumptions might she have made?

"Maybe," my client said, "the woman didn't actually have the information she needed and was trying to assert control. Maybe she was overcompensating. Maybe she felt threatened." We brainstormed possibilities—not to excuse the behavior, but to expand the lens.

That's when I saw it: my client had been responding as the expert. Her instinct, like mine used to be, was to lead with knowledge, to assert her credibility, to prove she belonged in the room.

But leadership at the executive level isn't just about what you know. It's about what you perceive, what you signal, and how you build trust in the face of friction.

Her emotional intelligence wasn't lacking—it was misapplied. She had mistaken emotional containment for emotional awareness. She believed that staying calm was the goal, rather than tuning in to her emotions.

That moment reminded me of my own calibration conversation with my own executive coach—the moment I realized that what I called professionalism was often fear in disguise.

We closed the session by reframing what a "successful" meeting outcome could look like. Not just technical clarity, but relational clarity, not just being right, but building rapport, not just leaving with answers, but leaving with alignment.

Chapter 6

For her, that shift—from proving to connecting—was the beginning of real emotional intelligence.

The Cost of Composure

We often praise leaders who remain composed under pressure. But for many women of color, composure isn't just a leadership trait—it's a survival tactic.

As I listened to my client recount her story—the tense meeting, the rapid-fire questions, her internal frustration—I recognized something deeply familiar. In both the situation and in her response. She had stayed calm. She hadn't interrupted. She waited for her turn. She told herself she was modeling professionalism. But underneath that steady exterior, her heart was racing. She was livid, and she was holding it all in.

I've been there.

I know what it feels like to be in a room where raising your voice—even slightly—might be interpreted as aggression. Where asking a pointed question is labeled as confrontational. Where being passionate about your position is misread as being too emotional.

Instead, we armor up with composure.

We nod. We wait. We take notes. We prepare well. We recite our credentials in our head like a mantra. And we remain silent—not because we have nothing to say, but because we're calculating the cost of saying it.

What I've learned, through my own experience and through coaching others, is that this version of composure has a price. It can cost us relationships, influence, and peace. Most of all, it can cost us our authenticity.

Too often, we confuse emotional intelligence with emotional suppression. We think being emotionally intelligent means being unbothered. We conflate professionalism with passivity. The truth is, emotional intelligence is not about holding your emotions hostage—it's about knowing what you feel, why you feel it, and how to respond in a way that aligns with your values and your leadership goals.

Chapter 6

And that includes honoring emotion—not erasing it.

There's another layer here, one I couldn't ignore as I coached my client through her story: the racialized expectations of professionalism. For Black women, and many women of color, the pressure to be emotionally controlled is not just internal—it's institutional. We know that anger can be weaponized against us. We've watched others be labeled "difficult" for showing too much feeling. So, we choose the safety of composure.

Sometimes, what we believe is "safe" is actually stifling.

As my client began to unpack the different interpretations of her silence—how the other woman may have seen her as cold, disconnected, or disengaged—it struck her that her efforts to appear unshaken may have come at the expense of true connection. She wasn't just protecting herself from judgment—she was also cutting herself off from the opportunity to build relational trust.

That realization opened the door to a new question: What would it look like to lead with presence instead of just composure?

That's the work of mastering emotional intelligence —learning how to manage your emotions and understanding how your emotional responses shape relationships, influence perception, and define your leadership presence.

It's not about being emotionless. It's about being emotionally aware.

That awareness has to be intersectional. It must account for how race, gender, power, and culture intersect with how we are allowed to express ourselves—and how we learn to express ourselves.

Because for many of us—especially Black women—professionalism isn't just about performance. It is about protection.

If we want to lead fully, honestly, and boldly—we have to let go of the version of professionalism that taught us our feelings were liabilities.

They are not.

Our feelings are data.
Our responses are choices.

Chapter 6

And our power lies in learning how to use both—wisely and well.

The Three Stories Coaching Tool: *Reclaiming Meaning in the Moment*

In high-stakes moments, our minds move fast. We replay scenes, assign motives, and make meaning based on instinct, memory, and emotion. Often, we walk away from a tough interaction with a single story about what happened—usually the one that protects our ego, confirms our fear, or reinforces what we've always believed.

What if that story isn't the whole truth?

Over the years, I've used a tool—first as a client, then in my coaching practice—that has helped clients untangle emotional moments with more clarity and less judgment. I call it *The Three Stories*. It's simple. It's transformative.

Here's how it works:

① *The Story You Tell Yourself*

This is the narrative you construct immediately after the event.

> "I was professional."
>
> "I handled it well."
>
> "They were out of line."

This story usually reflects your intent—what you meant to do, or what you hoped came across. It's often rooted in self-protection, pride, or identity.

② *The Story the Other Person Might Tell*

This one is harder. It requires you to step outside of yourself and imagine what the other person might have experienced.

> "She didn't say anything—maybe she was disengaged."
>
> "He cut me off—maybe he didn't respect my role."

It's not about assuming the worst. It's about acknowledging that silence, body language, or tone can be interpreted in ways we never intended.

③ *The Possible Truth in the Middle*

This is the gray space—the most powerful space. It's where self-awareness meets empathy. Where multiple perspectives can coexist.

It's often something like:

Chapter 6

"I was trying to stay composed. However, my silence might have created confusion. Maybe I could've clarified my intent or asked for a pause to reset the conversation."

The goal isn't to invalidate your experience. It's to **broaden your awareness** so you can move forward with more emotional agility, relational clarity, and strategic presence.

I first introduced this framework during a session with a brilliant, accomplished client who was sure she'd done everything right in a difficult meeting. On the surface, she had—she'd remained calm, didn't interrupt, and laid out her points logically.

As we unpacked the interaction using this tool, it became clear that her silence—intended as professionalism—could have been misread as disinterest, distance, or even passive resistance. And that realization shifted everything.

She wasn't "wrong." She was incomplete.

Once she saw the other possible stories, she could return to the relationship with more curiosity, more presence, and more intention. That's when real leadership begins—not when we're certain we're right, but when we're brave enough to explore what else might be true.

Reflection:

Think back to a recent difficult interaction.

- What was the story you told yourself?
- What might the other person's story be?
- What's the truth that might live between those two?

When tensions rise or a conversation goes sideways, our brains reach for a story—something to help us make sense of what just happened. But often, the first story we tell ourselves is incomplete.

The Three Stories Framework helps leaders reflect on challenging moments by exploring three possible interpretations.

This is where emotional intelligence meets empathy. It's not about blame—it's about growth.

Story #1: The Story You Tell Yourself
- Based on your intentions and how you want to be perceived
- Often serves to validate or protect your identity—but may ignore the impact of your actions

Story #3: The Possible Truth in the Middle
- Acknowledges nuance and opens the door to mutual understanding
- Where emotional intelligence meets empathy
- Not about blame—it's about growth

Story #2: The Story the Other Person Might Tell
- Centers on how your behavior may have been interpreted, regardless of intent
- Challenges you to think beyond your view and build relational awareness

Diagram 3: The Three Stories Framework

The Five Domains of Emotional Intelligence

The concept of emotional intelligence (EQ) is often referenced, but rarely broken down in meaningful, applicable ways. Daniel Goleman's research introduced five domains that help us move beyond the surface-level understanding of EQ as simply "being nice" or "staying calm." These domains work together to form the foundation of emotionally intelligent leadership.

Each one—self-awareness, self-regulation, motivation, empathy, and social skills—builds upon the others. In the next sections, we'll explore each of these components through real-life examples, coaching reflections, and leadership insights.

Self-Awareness: *The Power of Noticing*

Self-awareness is the cornerstone of emotional intelligence. It's the quiet, powerful practice of recognizing what you feel, when you feel it, and why. It's not about perfect control—it's about honest noticing.

And it's the hardest place to start, especially for high achievers.

When I first began working with my executive coach, I didn't realize how little space I gave myself to feel. I could name my goals, I could map out a strategy, but ask me to identify my emotions in real time? I'd freeze—or worse, I'd deflect with logic.

I remember once, in a debrief, my coach asked, "What did that moment feel like?"

Chapter 6

I rattled off what happened instead. "Well, I presented the data, and they said…"

She gently interrupted. "No, what did it feel like?"

I paused. Because I didn't know. I could recall what I said, what they said and how I responded. I didn't register what was happening inside my body. My voice had been steady, my tone neutral. But my stomach had been in knots the whole time.

That's when I realized: I had trained myself to bypass discomfort. To present as unbothered. And I mistook that for strength.

Self-awareness isn't about narrating your feelings out loud—it's about being connected enough to your emotional state that you can respond with intention instead of instinct. It's noticing the tension in your jaw before it becomes sarcasm. It's hearing your inner critic and choosing not to let her drive. It's saying to yourself, "I'm feeling dismissed right now," and deciding what to do about it from a place of clarity, not reactivity.

In coaching sessions, I often invite clients to pause

and do a simple scan:

- What am I feeling?
- Where am I feeling it in my body?
- What story am I telling myself right now?

These three questions—simple as they seem—often surface more truth than a 20-minute monologue. Because they cut through the noise and bring you back to what matters: your emotional reality.

The more you practice this, the faster your inner cues become visible. You start to recognize when a conversation triggers fear, or when a compliment makes you shrink instead of shine. And once you see those patterns, you can choose a new way to show up.

That is the first step to emotional intelligence. It's also the first step to emotional power.

Self-Regulation: *Responding, Not Reacting*

If self-awareness is the practice of noticing what you feel, self-regulation is what you do with what you feel.

It's not about suppressing emotion. It's about staying

Chapter 6

connected to it long enough to choose your response—especially in high-stakes, high-pressure moments when your leadership is most visible.

For years, I believed I was good at self-regulation because I rarely raised my voice. I didn't cry at work. I didn't let people "get to me." I kept my cool.

What I eventually learned was that composure isn't the same as control.

And silence isn't the same as strategy.

In one of my early leadership roles, a colleague made a backhanded comment about the way I spoke in meetings—specifically, my Southern accent. She smiled when she said it, as if it were harmless. "You're so polished," she said. "But sometimes the way you say things—it's very... regional."

I remember everything in my body tensing up. I wanted to clap back. I wanted to educate her. But instead, I smiled. I made a joke. I changed the subject.

I told myself I was "being professional."

Later that night, I couldn't sleep. My mind was

racing—not just with what I wish I'd said, but with all the moments I had minimized myself in the name of professionalism. That moment didn't just sting—it stuck.

It was my executive coach who helped me see it differently.

She asked, "What story are you telling yourself about your response?"

I told her that staying calm meant I had control of the situation.

She nodded. "Or did it mean you didn't feel safe enough to respond?"

That landed hard. Because the truth was—I didn't. And that's not weakness. That's data.

Self-regulation isn't about pretending you're okay. It's about learning how to honor your emotional experience and make choices that align with your values, your goals, and your power.

Sometimes, those choices include naming the discomfort in real time—with clarity and care.

One of the most useful tools I've shared with clients

Chapter 6

is something I learned from the book *Difficult Conversations*—the SBI model:

Situation. Behavior. Impact.

It helps you offer honest feedback, especially when a moment triggers insecurity, frustration, or pain.

If I could go back to that moment—when my colleague made the "regional" comment about my accent—here's how I might have responded using SBI:

"When we were in the meeting earlier and you commented on my professionalism, and then said that sometimes I say things that are 'regional'—it made me feel a bit insecure about my accent. I just wanted to check—was that what you intended to convey?"

It's short. It's honest. And it opens the door to dialogue without immediately assigning blame.

You don't have to be perfect to be emotionally intelligent. You just have to be present—and willing to tell the truth.

Sometimes the most emotionally intelligent thing

you can do is say:

"Hey, that didn't sit right with me. Can we talk about it?"

That's self-regulation in action. Not silence. Not compliance. But a choice to speak from your core, not your armor.

Motivation: *Leading from Within*

Motivation, in the context of emotional intelligence, isn't about raw ambition. It's about being driven by something deeper than titles, status, or external validation. It's the fire that burns quietly beneath your professional identity—the why behind the what.

For many leaders I coach, especially those who've risen by mastering their technical skills, motivation often starts as a quest to prove themselves. We want to show we're capable. We want to exceed expectations. We want to silence the doubt in our own heads—and sometimes in the eyes of others.

I know that pattern well. Early in my career, I was always chasing the next rung. I was proud of what I'd accomplished. However, I thought I had to constantly do more to be seen as enough. I wasn't driven by purpose—I was driven by pressure.

It wasn't until much later, through reflection and coaching, that I asked myself a powerful question: **What would I do if I weren't trying to prove anything to anyone?**

That question changed everything. It shifted my motivation from external to internal, from fear to focus, from hustle to alignment.

When your motivation is rooted in internal clarity—your values, your purpose, your long-term vision—it sustains you through challenges. It doesn't mean you stop being ambitious. It means your ambition is anchored.

I once coached a leader who had checked all the boxes: graduate degree, prestigious role, visible success. Yet, she felt empty. "I've been climbing a ladder," she said, "but I'm not even sure it's leaning against the right building."

So, we got curious together. What mattered to her

now? What legacy did she want to leave? What brought her joy—not just what brought her praise?

As we peeled back the layers, she realized her motivation had always been about safety. Achievement had been her shield. But she didn't want a life defined by constant defense—she wanted one defined by deliberate impact.

That's what motivation as an emotional intelligence skill invites us to examine: not just what we're doing, but why.

The emotionally intelligent leader is one who can say:
- "I know what I'm working toward."
- "I'm willing to redefine success if it no longer aligns with my truth."
- "I move with intention—not just momentum."

When your motivation is aligned with your values, you don't just move faster—you move wiser.

Chapter 6

Empathy: *Feeling Beyond Your Frame*

Empathy is the bridge between self-awareness and social awareness. It's the ability to feel with others—not just for them—and to understand experiences outside of your own. In leadership, empathy doesn't mean taking on everyone's emotions or being overly accommodating. It means being attuned to what people need, even when they can't name it themselves.

It's also what helps us lead with humanity instead of hierarchy.

During the coaching session I shared earlier, when my client described the barrage of questions she faced in her meeting, she was understandably focused on her own experience. She felt disrespected, caught off guard, and misjudged. Her first instinct was to hold her ground and assert her technical expertise—because that's where she felt safest.

As we explored the Three Stories tool, something shifted. She began to consider what might have been driving the other woman's behavior. What pressures she could've been under. What fears she may have been managing. What insecurities might have been masked by her assertiveness.

That moment—when my client could acknowledge her own hurt and still hold space for someone else's possible reality—that was empathy.

Empathy expands the conversation. It invites nuance. It shifts us out of "me versus you" and into "what's really happening between us?"

One of the most emotionally intelligent things a leader can do is pause in conflict and ask:
- "What might this person be experiencing right now?"
- "What could be underneath their tone, questions, or silence?"
- "What's the story behind the story?"

Empathy doesn't mean excusing harm. It doesn't mean tolerating disrespect. But it does mean choosing curiosity over certainty. Especially in moments of tension.

When we lead with empathy, we stop reacting to people's behavior and start responding to their humanity.

That's when trust is built. That's when transformation begins.

Social Skills: *Influence Without Authority*

Social skills are the outward expression of emotional intelligence. They are how your internal awareness, regulation, motivation, and empathy translate into how you lead, collaborate, resolve conflict, and influence people.

In leadership, social skills are not about being charismatic or extroverted. They're about being effective in relationships—up, down, and across. It's about knowing how to listen, how to adapt, how to hold space for hard conversations, and how to build trust even when power dynamics are complex.

One of the most overlooked aspects of social skill is what I call "reading the room without losing yourself in it." The emotionally intelligent leader doesn't just watch for verbal cues—they're also tuned in to energy, pacing, dynamics, and unspoken norms. They know when to speak, when to pause, and when to invite others in.

I worked with a senior leader who had incredible technical expertise and was deeply respected for her knowledge. When she stepped into a new executive role, she struggled to build alliances with her peers. "I feel like I'm saying all the right things," she told me, "yet, nothing seems to land."

As we worked together, it became clear that she was delivering information—not connection. Her communication style was efficient, precise, and technically sound—however, it lacked warmth and presence. Once we layered in emotional cues, active listening, and some simple relationship-building habits, everything shifted. People didn't just hear her —they began to trust her.

That's the power of social skill. It's not manipulation. It's mastery of relational awareness.

Here are a few questions emotionally intelligent leaders ask themselves when navigating relationships:

- "Am I building connection, or just delivering content?"
- "Have I created space for others to feel seen and heard?"
- "Do I know how my presence affects the room?"

Social skills are what help you move things forward—through relationships, not through force. They allow you to challenge without alienating, to give feedback without triggering shame, and to motivate without coercing.

When all the other domains of emotional intelligence come together, social skill is what people experience. It's how they remember you. And ultimately, it's how your leadership legacy is shaped.

Common Misconceptions About Emotional Intelligence

Despite the growing emphasis on emotional intelligence (EQ), misunderstandings about what it truly is—and isn't—remain widespread. These misconceptions are especially prominent among women.

One of the most persistent myths is that emotional intelligence means staying calm at all costs. That it requires leaders to remain unshaken, agreeable, and composed—even in the face of conflict. For women, this belief is often reinforced by unspoken expectations to be accommodating, emotionally restrained, and to manage the tone of the room.

This is not emotional intelligence. It's emotional labor.

Another myth is that emotional intelligence means being soft or passive—that it's about avoiding conflict rather than navigating it. Real EQ isn't about being agreeable. It's about being intentional, present, and responsive.

For women—especially those navigating predominantly white, male-dominated, or hierarchical workplaces—emotional suppression is often misread as professionalism. Suppression is not mastery. Awareness is. Integration is. Courage is.

True emotional intelligence invites us to show up

more fully, not less, to name the unspoken, to lead with clarity and care.

DOMAIN	COMMON MISCONCEPTIONS	ACTUAL PRACTICE
Self-Awareness	Knowing how you *should* feel	Recognizing your actual emotional patterns
Self-Regulation	Suppressing your emotions	Managing your responses with intention
Motivation	Proving your worth	Acting from internal purpose and values
Empathy	Being overly emotional	Understanding and connecting to others' emotions
Social Skills	Being liked or agreeable	Building trust and influence through relationships

Table 4: Visual Guide to Common Misconceptions v. Actual Practice

Reflection

Emotional intelligence is not a fixed trait—it's a skill. And like any skill, it grows with practice, feedback, and self-honesty.

As you reflect, consider the following questions:

- Which of the five domains do you feel strongest in right now?
- Which domain do you avoid or downplay?
- When was the last time you practiced emotional intelligence under pressure?
- What would it look like to show up with more emotional presence?

Leadership in Action

Choose one domain to focus on over the next 30 days. Here are a few practice ideas:

- Keep a journal to track emotional patterns and triggers.
- Use the SBI model (Situation–Behavior–Impact) in hard conversations.

- Invite feedback from trusted colleagues about how you show up.
- Focus on building connection, not just delivering expertise.

"Emotional intelligence is not about being unshaken. It's about being aware, responsive, and rooted in who you are—even when the room tells you to be someone else."

—Dr. Tammi Fleming

Want to Go Deeper?

Turn to your companion guide and complete the guided reflection: *EQ in Action: 30 Days of Intentional Leadership*. Use the space provided to select your focus domain and track small daily shifts in practice, perspective, and presence.

This companion guide is available for purchase at: **www.diamondconsultantsllc.com**

Part III:
Stepping into Leadership with Intention

Chapter 7
Owning Your Voice & Executive Presence

More Than a Look, It's a Leadership Language

I didn't always know what executive presence was—but I knew when I didn't feel it.

I didn't feel it in the rooms where I rehearsed my words in my head and never said them aloud. I didn't feel it in the moments where my accent made me shrink, not shine. I didn't feel it the day I realized I had more credentials than half the people at the table, yet still questioned whether I belonged there.

The concept of executive presence was never explicitly taught to me—not in school, not in trainings, and certainly not in the early days of my career. I learned, through lived experience, that presence isn't just how others see you. It's how you see yourself—and how that self-image holds up under pressure.

It's the energy you bring into a room before you say

a word. The weight your silence carries. The calm in your questions. The impact of your pause.

For years, I thought presence was reserved for the powerful—for people with fancy titles, flawless diction, and polished confidence. What I've learned is this: presence isn't about performance. It's about permission. Giving yourself permission to lead from your truth—not someone else's template.

In this chapter, I want to share what I've learned about how others experience presence and how you cultivate it for yourself. I'll unpack the myths, the mindset shifts, and the quiet power that presence can hold. Because the truth is, your voice matters. Your visibility matters. And your vibe, that's your leadership language.

Let's talk about how to own all of it—on purpose.

Common Myths About Executive Presence: *What It's Not, and What It Is*

Before we can fully embrace executive presence, we have to unlearn some of the noise around it.

Chapter 7

Executive presence is often wrapped in vague expectations and coded language—especially for women, people of color, and professionals from nontraditional backgrounds. It gets described as "polish," "gravitas," or "commanding the room"—but those descriptions often do more to confuse than clarify.

Let's name some of the myths.

Myth #1: Executive presence is about being the loudest voice in the room.

Truth: Presence isn't about volume. It's about resonance. The most powerful leaders I've worked with rarely raise their voice—yet, when they speak, people lean in. Presence shows up in your clarity, your timing, and your ability to create space, not dominate it.

Myth #2: Executive presence means dressing a certain way.

Truth: Style can support presence. It doesn't define it. What matters more is alignment—does your appearance reflect who you are and how you want to be experienced? Presence is about congruence, not conformity. You don't need a power suit to carry power.

Myth #3: You either have executive presence or you don't.

Truth: Executive presence is not a fixed trait—it's a skill you build. It's shaped by self-awareness, practice, and intentionality. It evolves as you evolve. And like any skill, it can be strengthened over time.

Myth #4: It's only for senior leaders.

Truth: Presence isn't tied to your title—it's tied to your impact. I've seen interns with executive presence and senior leaders without it. It's about how you show up in your role, not the rank you hold.

Myth #5: You need to perform with confidence at all times.

Truth: Real presence allows space for vulnerability. You can be composed and unsure. You can ask for help and still be seen as a leader. Presence isn't about having all the answers—it's about how you navigate uncertainty with grace and grounding.

Chapter 7

MYTH	TRUTH
You have to be the loudest voice in the room.	Presence is about resonance, not volume.
It's all about how you dress.	Style can enhance-but presence comes from alignment, not appearance.
You either have it or you don't.	Executive presence is a skill you can learn and strengthen over time.
Only senior leaders have executive presence.	Anyone, at any level, can lead with presence—it's about impact, not title.
You must always appear confident and polished.	Presence includes vulnerability. It's about composure, not perfection.

Table 5: The Myths and Truths of Executive Presence

Cultivating Influence and Presence: *Voice, Visibility, and Vibe*

Executive presence isn't about charisma or

perfection. It's about alignment. It's about being rooted in who you are, intentional about how you show up, and aware of how others experience you.

When I coach leaders on presence, I often break it down into three core components: voice, visibility, and vibe.

Voice: Your Clarity and Conviction

Your voice is more than the sound of your words—it's the clarity behind your thoughts, the calm in your delivery, and the conviction with which you speak.

For years, I thought speaking up meant talking more. But the executive voice is strategic. It's about knowing what matters, when to speak, and how to say it in a way that elevates the conversation.

I once coached a leader who felt invisible in meetings. She'd done all the prep work, had the data, the insights—yet, she rarely spoke up. When she did, her voice would trail off. We worked together to identify what was holding her back, and she realized it wasn't lack of knowledge—it was the fear of being dismissed. Once she began speaking with clarity and

Chapter 7

pausing with intention, her voice carried farther: not louder—clearer. That's presence.

Ask yourself: Are you using your voice to inform, to influence, or to impress?

Visibility: Owning the Room Without Shrinking

Visibility isn't about spotlight-chasing. It's about owning your value—especially when no one's clapping.

Too often, brilliant leaders shrink in the spaces where they should be standing tall. They downplay their expertise, sit at the edge of the room, or wait to be invited in. Visibility is the decision to take up space—physically, intellectually, emotionally.

It's walking into a room and not asking for permission to matter.

I've worked with mid-career professionals who hesitate to claim credit for their work, fearing they'll appear arrogant. Visibility isn't arrogance—it's accountability. If your work matters, your presence should reflect that. Say your name. Own your role. And don't wait until you're 100% confident—walk in as if you're 100% worthy because you are.

Ask yourself: Where do I hesitate to be seen—and what would change if I stopped waiting?

Vibe: The Unspoken Power of Your Energy

Your vibe is the emotional atmosphere you create. It's how people feel when they're in your presence—and after you've left the room.

It's not just your words—it's your energy. Your tone. Your rhythm. Your ability to hold tension or offer calm. It's how grounded you are when others are spinning.

Vibe doesn't mean you're always happy or peaceful. It means you're anchored—that your leadership doesn't shake just because the situation does. The best leaders I know can project calm even in chaos, and presence even in silence. Their energy is steady, inviting, and clear.

In my federal role, I began to realize that vibe was one of my strongest assets. I could walk into tense cross-agency meetings and immediately sense the room's emotional temperature. I didn't rush to fix it

Chapter 7

—I adjusted my own energy first. Often, that was enough to shift the tone for everyone else.

Ask yourself: What energy do I bring into the room—and what do I leave behind?

Together, voice, visibility, and vibe create a kind of leadership gravity, not loud, not flashy, but undeniable.

You don't have to be the most impressive person in the room to have presence. You just need to show up fully aligned—with your words, your energy, and your worth.

 ## Reflection

Presence in Practice

Take a moment to reflect on how you're currently showing up in your professional spaces.
- Where is your voice strongest—and where do you hold back?
- Are there moments when you choose to shrink rather than be seen?

- What kind of energy are you bringing into the room?
- When you walk away, what do you hope people remember—your words, your wisdom, or your presence?

Presence isn't about performance. It's about being aligned with your truth.

You don't need to change who you are—you need to own who you are, fully and intentionally.

> *"I didn't always know how to bring all of myself into the room. But the moment I stepped into the highest levels of government, I had to decide—was I going to perform, or be present?"*
>
> —Dr. Tammi Fleming

Chapter 7

Bringing Presence into Power:
My Federal Appointment

After ten years in philanthropy, I made one of the biggest decisions of my career: I accepted an appointment with the Biden-Harris Administration as the Infrastructure Investment Equity Fellow at the U.S. Department of Labor. It was a proud moment. I knew I had the skills, the vision, and the drive. It was also a test—could I show up at the highest levels of government and lead with confidence, clarity, and presence?

I worked hard for this opportunity. I had earned my seat at the table. Now I had to occupy that seat—fully. I had to navigate executive spaces, work across agencies, and collaborate with the White House. There would be no easing in. The test would be immediate.

I did what I always do when I'm nervous—I studied. For two weeks before my first day, I immersed myself in the 600-page infrastructure plan and pored over agency organizational charts like I was preparing for a final exam. I needed to feel prepared. I needed to know the language.

Nothing could have prepared me for that first meeting.

It felt like I'd landed in a foreign country. Acronyms I'd never heard. A pace I wasn't used to. Conversations that moved so quickly it felt like every third word was code. My heart raced. My confidence wavered. It was a virtual meeting, and thank goodness so many folks had their cameras off, because I quickly turned mine off too—and took a deep breath.

Then I remembered something I'd worked so hard to internalize in the years leading up to this moment: **"You don't have to prove anything. You just have to be present."**

I turned my camera back on. And I listened.

I made a conscious decision at that moment: I wasn't going to perform. I wasn't going to scramble to sound smart. I wasn't going to try to prove I belonged in that room. I already knew I did.

Instead, I would contribute intentionally. I would

speak when it mattered. I would ask questions with purpose. I would lead with presence, not with performance.

It worked.

I stopped chasing the right answers. I started asking the right questions. I learned that inviting others to think more deeply was often more impactful than offering the quickest solution. Over time, I became known not for technical prowess—but for my ability to frame conversations, build trust, and bring people together.

Six months in, I was charged with designing the national equity strategy for the Department of Labor's infrastructure investments. I worked alongside program leaders across agencies, launched stakeholder engagements in thirteen states, and co-designed cross-functional teams. I traveled across the country as part of the U.S. Secretary of Labor's national implementation team.

Here's the part that surprised me most: I was no longer doing the technical work.

The woman who once prided herself on knowing all the answers had stopped doing—and started leading.

What made me effective wasn't just my content knowledge. It was my ability to see the big picture. To broker relationships between state and local government, workforce boards, community organizations, and unions. It was the energy I brought into the room. The way I listened before I spoke. The way I made space for others to shine.

And the trait I once felt most insecure about—my accent—became the thing that made people lean in. Over and over again, someone would pause mid-meeting and ask, "Where are you from?"

When I said, "New Orleans," I now noticed how the room would light up. Stories about favorite meals, music, family trips, Mardi Gras. The connection was instant.

The voice I once tried to soften—the one I thought made me sound "less than"—was now the one thing they remembered most. I didn't need to change who I was to lead in high places.

Chapter 7

I just had to bring all of me—intentionally and unapologetically.

Client Vignette:
Marlaina's Voice at the Executive Table

I once coached a brilliant woman named Marlaina who had just been promoted into a senior leadership role. She was strategic, deeply committed, and had earned the respect of her team. But the moment she stepped into cross-functional executive meetings, she froze.

Not physically—but vocally.

She'd prepare meticulously. Her notes were detailed, her insights sharp. But when it was time to speak, she hesitated. She second-guessed her thoughts. She deferred, even when she knew the answer. And after meetings, she'd replay the silence in her head, questioning why she hadn't spoken up.

During one session, Marlaina got quiet. Then she said, "The voice inside my head keeps saying, 'You're not ready.' And the longer I stay silent, the louder that voice gets."

She wasn't missing skills. She was managing internal doubt. That doubt wasn't just about her role—it was about how she was being perceived. She feared that speaking too directly, too passionately, or too early would make her seem aggressive or unpolished. She worried that her voice, shaped by culture, cadence, and conviction, wouldn't fit the mold of what executive presence was supposed to sound like.

I looked at her and said something I wish someone had told me early on: "Your voice doesn't need to be perfect. It needs to be present."

Together, we built a strategy rooted in small, intentional shifts. In every meeting, Marlaina committed to:
- Asking one thoughtful, clarifying question.
- Speaking one insight aloud—even if it wasn't perfectly worded.
- Affirming someone else's idea, and then expanding on it.

Chapter 7

She didn't need to dominate the conversation. She needed to trust her value in the room.

The transformation was undeniable.

Marlaina began speaking with intention, not anxiety. She paused with purpose. Her questions started shaping the direction of conversations. She was no longer waiting to be seen—she was showing up, fully and strategically.

By the end of the quarter, her presence had shifted the room. She wasn't just seen as a new leader. She was respected as a steady one, a thought partner, a voice people leaned toward.

Lessons from High-Level Spaces

There's something surreal about walking into rooms you once only read about—rooms filled with agency leaders, national foundations, political appointees, and even the high-level White House officials.

For years, I imagined there was a secret code—a tone, a pedigree, a way of speaking or carrying oneself—that made people worthy of those rooms. I thought there was a mold I hadn't yet fit, a polish I hadn't yet earned. I was certain that someone would eventually realize I didn't belong.

Here's what I've learned from actually being in those spaces:

The people who speak the loudest don't always have the most to say.

The ones with the longest titles don't always offer the clearest vision.

And the people who hold the most power often crave one thing: realness.

They want someone who doesn't just echo what sounds politically safe or strategically rehearsed—they want someone who can name what's not being said. Someone who can hold complexity, speak truth with grace, and create space for others to show up more honestly.

That's a kind of leadership presence you can't fake. It has to be cultivated.

One of my greatest lessons was: You don't need to perform your brilliance in high-level spaces. You need to own it.

Owning it doesn't mean talking over people. It doesn't mean dropping credentials like confetti. It doesn't even mean speaking first.

Sometimes, presence looks like:
- Asking the question no one wants to ask
- Naming what's sitting in the silence
- Holding the tension between what's said and what's felt
- Being the calmest person in the room when everything else is spinning

In my role as a federal appointee, I helped shape national equity strategy, facilitated politically charged conversations, and supported the implementation of billion-dollar investments. None of that would've mattered if I hadn't first grounded myself.

What made the difference wasn't my résumé—it was my rhythm.

It was how I read the room.

It was the way I listened.

It was my presence.

There were meetings where the dynamics were charged—where multiple agencies had conflicting priorities or where power struggles were quietly pulsing beneath the surface. In those moments, I didn't speak to prove I belonged. I spoke when the room needed grounding. I echoed what others were trying to say but couldn't quite articulate. I built trust by making others feel seen.

And what surprised me the most?

The less I tried to be impressive, the more others trusted me to lead.

Because when people feel safe around your presence, they become more open to your influence. That's the power of executive presence—it's not about being the loudest or the smartest.

Chapter 7

It's about being the most anchored.

Your presence is your strategy. Your energy is part of your influence. And your **authenticity is your edge.**

The Practice of Presence and Power

Executive presence isn't something you're born with. It's something you build—on purpose.

Not through performance, through **alignment**.
Not through perfection, through **intention**.

I used to think influence came from having all the answers. Now I know it comes from how you show up when the answers aren't clear.

Presence is your leadership language. It's how your values translate into action. It's how your voice becomes a tool, not just a sound. It's how your energy shifts a room, even when you say very little.

And influence? That comes when who you are, how you show up, and how others experience you are all in sync.

You don't need to:
- Speak the most
- Perform expertise
- Prove your intelligence
- Change your voice
- Shrink to make others comfortable
- Stretch to become something you're not

You need to trust your presence—and build it deliberately.

Here's what cultivating presence really looks like in action:
- **Self-Trust:** You no longer perform what you already know. You rest in it.
- **Clarity:** You speak with intention, not excess. You make your point, then make space for others.
- **Restraint:** You don't need to interrupt or rush. You understand the weight of well-timed silence.
- **Consistency:** You bring the same energy across spaces—not a performance, but a practice.

- **Permission:** You stop waiting for someone to invite you in. You walk in, anchored in who you are.

That's the essence of presence.

It's not about being the loudest voice. It's about being the **clearest signal** in the noise.

It's not about commanding the room. It's about creating a space where others can think, breathe, and follow your lead.

It's not about image. It's about **impact**.

Call to Action: A Small Act of Confidence

Executive presence isn't built in grand gestures—it's shaped in the small, consistent choices you make every day.

Every meeting, every conversation, every moment of doubt is an opportunity to lead from alignment instead of anxiety.

You don't need a title to step into presence.
You don't need a spotlight to influence.
You don't need permission to take up space.

You just need a single, intentional act of confidence —and the courage to repeat it.

This week, practice showing up with purpose in three simple ways:

Voice
- Speak up in a moment when silence feels safer.
- Ask a question that deepens the conversation instead of closing it.
- Share your perspective with clarity, even if it goes against the grain.

Visibility
- Take a seat at the main table—literally or figuratively.
- Introduce yourself with presence. Say your name like it belongs in the room.
- Volunteer to present, contribute, or represent —even if your voice shakes.

Vibe
- Check your energy before entering a space. What do you want to bring in?

- Breathe before you speak. Lead from calm, not urgency.
- Let your presence anchor the room—not your need to be heard, but your intention to be felt.

Then reflect:
- What shifted when you showed up with intention?
- How did the room change—or how did you?
- What do you want your presence to say before you speak?

Executive presence isn't a performance.

It's not about commanding attention.

It's about embodying who you are—with clarity, confidence, and care.

You already have the power.

Now—use it, one bold choice at a time.

Owning Your Voice & Executive Presence

 ## Reflection

Presence isn't how loud you speak—it's how fully you show up.

- What's one space this week where you will lead with more intention?
- What's one part of yourself you've been hiding that you're ready to bring forward?

Want to Go Deeper?

Let's put presence into practice.

If this chapter challenged you to reflect on how you're showing up—and what you're holding back—**The Leadership Detour Companion Guide** offers targeted prompts, exercises, and a coaching tool to help you clarify your voice, strengthen your presence, and lead with more intention.

Download your digital copy at
www.diamondconsultantsllc.com

Chapter 7

"*I will not shrink so you can feel tall. I will rise—and invite you to rise too.*"

—Dr. Tammi Fleming

Chapter 8
Building a Leadership Mindset for the Long Game

Thinking Beyond Today

When my presidential appointment with the Biden-Harris Administration ended, I was offered the opportunity to return to my former agency. On paper, it made sense. I'd spent over a decade there. I knew the work, the people, the culture. The role came with a comfortable salary, great benefits, and a seamless transition back into familiar territory.

However, something in me felt uneasy.

At first, I couldn't name it. But as I sat with the offer, the feeling grew louder. Despite two years of success—working across federal, state, and local systems, designing national strategy, earning the trust of top leaders—the thought of going back made my chest tighten.

I had to ask myself: What was this anxiety really about?

Chapter 8

The answer was humbling.

It wasn't just the work. It was the idea of going back to a space where I still felt I had something to prove. A space where I might shrink, default, perform. I'd spent years growing into the woman who could lead with clarity, confidence, and calm. Going back meant returning to a version of me I'd outgrown.

I didn't want to do that—not even for a comfortable paycheck.

For the first time, I chose to listen to the part of me that wasn't afraid, but clear.

I didn't have another job lined up. I didn't have a safety net. But I had vision.

I had purpose.

I had me.

I declined the offer. I made a decision that would shift my life entirely: I would step fully into my legacy work.

When Success Becomes a Cage

How do you walk away from something others would kill for?

I had the offer in hand, a secure role, a generous salary, full benefits, and a familiar environment. For many, it was the dream scenario—a golden ticket back into comfort.

Something didn't feel right. I couldn't ignore it.

On the surface, the job made perfect sense. I'd done the work before. I knew the systems. I had credibility. The transition would be smooth, predictable, safe.

Underneath, I could feel the tension building in my chest.

That's when I realized: comfort can be a kind of cage.

I wasn't just deciding whether to take a job. I was wrestling with what it meant to choose safety over alignment—and the emotional weight that comes with that kind of decision.

A colleague once called it the golden handcuffs—the allure of high pay, generous benefits, and perceived prestige that keep you tethered to roles you've long outgrown. The truth is, many of us wear them with a smile. We convince ourselves we should be grateful, even when the cost is high. We trade authenticity for access. We carry titles that weigh more than they're worth.

For me, part of the struggle was financial. After 30 years of steady paychecks, I knew exactly what would land in my bank account every two weeks. I knew how to plan. I knew how to save. That kind of certainty is a privilege—and walking away from it felt terrifying.

Deeper than that was something harder to name: Imposter syndrome wrapped in achievement.

Even with years of experience and a national appointment under my belt, part of me whispered, "What if this is the best offer you ever get?"
"What if this was luck, not leadership?"
"What if no one else will pay you this much to be you?"

That's how you stay stuck.

Not because you're lazy.

But because fear puts on a suit and calls itself "practical."

I started asking myself questions I'd avoided for months:
- If I say yes, what part of me do I have to silence?
- How much of my energy will go into wearing the mask?
- Will I be leading—or just performing leadership again?

The emotional cost of comfort is real. It asks you to shrink your vision in exchange for stability. It asks you to manage your image more than your impact. And sometimes, it convinces you that the very thing you've earned is just a fluke—that you should hang onto it before someone realizes you're not supposed to have it.

That's not leadership. That's survival with benefits.

I made a different choice.

I said no.

Not because I didn't need the money. Not because I

had another offer lined up. But because I was finally more committed to my purpose than my performance. I wanted to build something of my own—not return to a space that still asked me to prove I belonged.

And that kind of clarity? That's the real freedom.

What Barbara Taught Me About Clarity and the Long Game

When I think about what it means to lead with vision—to hold steady through uncertainty, to resist the pull of comfort in favor of something bigger—I think of Barbara.

She wasn't trained in strategy. She didn't have a title. She had vision. She had clarity. And she had the kind of patience that most of us only develop after being told "no" enough times to stop asking—and start building.

I remember being a child in the St. Thomas Housing Development in New Orleans when Barbara and other community leaders organized the rent strike to protest the unlivable conditions we were forced to endure.

The buildings were crumbling, mold spread through apartments like ivy, and safety felt like a luxury—not a right. Leadership was growing in those same cracks. And Barbara? She stood in the center of those cracks—where leadership was rising and community power was taking root.

It wasn't just a one-day protest. It was a calculated, sustained movement. As documented years later by Tulane University in *The Cost of Home*, the rent strike—led by the St. Thomas Resident Council—culminated in a takeover of the Housing Authority of New Orleans' main office. They demanded to be heard. Eventually, they were. The strike led to a **$21 million rehabilitation grant from U.S. Department of Housing and Urban Development**.

That didn't happen overnight. Barbara knew it wouldn't.

She knew what was at stake. She knew the backlash could be swift. She knew the threat of eviction hung over all of us like a storm cloud. She stood anyway, for herself—for her children, her neighbors—and for

Chapter 8

her people.

She understood something I didn't have the language for back then:

Change doesn't come from reaction. It comes from resolve.

She played the long game.

Even though I was too young to grasp the depth of what was happening, I felt the weight of it. I watched her steady herself for a fight that wouldn't end in a news cycle. I saw her organize food drives, community meetings, strategy sessions—quiet forms of power that rarely make headlines yet it shifts entire systems.

Years later, when I sat with the offer to return to my former agency—complete with its comfort, familiarity, and financial security—I kept thinking about Barbara. About how she didn't strike for comfort. She struck for change, for dignity, for something better.

I realized I had a decision to make, too—not about housing policy, but about how I wanted to lead my own life.

Was I willing to sit in uncertainty for a vision I believed in?

Was I prepared to endure short-term discomfort for long-term alignment?

Could I say no to what was easy, in service of what was right—for me?

That was the moment I understood that this wasn't just a career decision. It was a leadership one.

Barbara didn't teach me how to plan my five-year goals. She taught me how to stand in clarity when fear is loud. How to make decisions not from desperation—but from direction. How to take a breath, hold your ground, and trust that a better outcome is possible—even if you can't see it yet.

Her leadership shaped the way I view mine:

Not just as a role. As a responsibility.

Not as something reactive. As something intentional.

Not for the moment—but for the movement ahead.

Barbara never called it "long-game strategy." But

Chapter 8

that's exactly what it was.

Now, decades later, I finally understand what she was modeling.

Leadership isn't about how quickly you win. It's about how deeply you believe that the win is worth the wait.

Client Story:
When Climbing No Longer Feels Like Success

Just a few months after I stepped into my purpose, I was coaching a client—let's call her Aisha—who was navigating a similar crossroads.

She had just been promoted into a highly visible leadership role. The kind of role she had worked toward for years. It came with a salary bump, a corner office, and a seat at the executive table. From the outside, she had made it.

In our sessions, something deeper kept surfacing. She felt disconnected, tired, uninspired, and ashamed for feeling that way.

"I should be happy," she told me, her voice tight with

frustration. "I know how many people would kill for this job. But I don't feel like I'm leading. I feel like I'm going through the motions."

Aisha wasn't ungrateful. She was **out of alignment**.

She'd spent so much of her career climbing—proving, pushing, excelling—that when she reached the top, she realized she'd been chasing someone else's version of success. She didn't want more meetings, more status, or more visibility. She wanted meaning. She wanted to build. She wanted to make decisions that reflected who she had become—not who she was five years ago.

Like so many leaders, she was stuck in the tension between gratitude and growth. Between what looked good on paper—and what felt right in her spirit.

We spent weeks unpacking that. Not rushing toward a decision. Just sitting with the discomfort. Naming what no longer fit. Creating space to dream about what might come next if she led herself from vision instead of fear.

Eventually, she made a bold move. She did not quit. She redesigned her role. She restructured her team.

Chapter 8

She shifted her time to focus on strategy and mentorship. She started building the kind of legacy she wanted to leave, right where she was.

The difference was night and day. She wasn't just showing up. She was alive again.

Her story reminded me that legacy work doesn't always start with walking away. Sometimes, it begins by telling the truth about what success no longer means—and reclaiming your right to lead from purpose.

 **Reflection**

What Are You Choosing for the Long Game?

Barbara didn't just make noise—she made a plan. She modeled what it looks like to choose clarity over comfort, direction over distraction.

Now it's your turn to reflect.

Take 10–15 minutes to journal or sit with these questions:

- Where in your life are you being called to lead with more clarity?

- What decision are you postponing because fear feels easier than vision?
- Have you ever stayed in something too long—because it looked good on paper?
- What would it mean to make a decision today that your future self would thank you for?

"The hardest part of long-game leadership isn't the decision—it's the discipline to trust it."

—Dr. Tammi Fleming

What are you willing to trust today?

The Emotional Toll of Unclear Leadership

It's easy to talk about clarity like it's a light switch—something you flip on when the timing is right. But most of the time, it's a slow unraveling. And when it's missing, the cost is far more than professional.

I've worked with high-performing leaders who have mastered the art of holding it together while falling apart inside. They show up. They deliver. They're the go-to. Underneath the surface, there's a current of exhaustion, not from overwork. The exhaustion is from operating without direction.

That's what unclear leadership feels like.

You're not lost. You're just unmoored.

You're not failing. You're just unsure of what success actually means now.

You're not ungrateful. You're just craving alignment —and you don't know how to name it.

Unclear leadership doesn't always look chaotic. In fact, it often wears the mask of competence. While inside, it feels like:
- Constant second-guessing
- Saying yes out of fear, not conviction
- Performing confidence while quietly panicking
- Watching others celebrate your life while you feel invisible in it.

Over time, that disconnect becomes unsustainable.

When I think about the seasons in my career that drained me the most, they weren't the ones where I was busiest. They were the ones where I had no clarity. Where I was doing work that no longer matched who I was becoming. Where I was chasing external validation because I had no internal compass.

That kind of leadership doesn't just dull your impact—it slowly erodes your sense of self.

One client once told me, "I don't hate my job—I just don't recognize myself in it anymore."

That's the toll.

When we lead without vision, we start to lose our own reflection in the process. We forget what we value. We say yes to things we don't believe in. We stay in roles that make us smaller. We start calling survival "strategy."

Eventually, the body catches up.

Burnout. Numbness. Short temper. Restlessness. Doubt disguised as diligence.

But when we re-anchor ourselves in clarity—when we slow down, ask the real questions, and get honest about what we need—everything begins to shift.

You can't build a sustainable career—or a healthy life

Chapter 8

—on a foundation of uncertainty.

You have to define what you're building.

You have to name what matters.

You have to reclaim the why behind the what.

Clarity isn't just a leadership tool. It's a form of self-preservation.

And when you find it, protect it—because your leadership depends on it.

From Climbing to Clarity

Aisha's story stayed with me.

Because for a long time, I measured leadership the same way she did—by the climb.

Each new role felt like validation. Each title, a stamp of progress. For years, that thinking served me well. It gave me structure, ambition, and something to strive for.

Eventually, I started asking different questions:
- I stopped asking, *"What's next?"* And started asking, *"What matters most?"*

- I stopped asking, *"How do I get there?"* And started wondering, *"Why do I want to go there at all?"*

This is what happens when you shift from chasing roles to building a legacy.

You stop defining success by how high you can go—and start measuring it by what you're building, who you're impacting, and how your leadership is making life better for others.

Legacy work isn't about the spotlight. It's about alignment—with your values, your purpose, and your vision.

It requires a different mindset, a slower pace, a deeper level of intention.

You start evaluating opportunities by their fit, not by their title or by the paycheck. You ask:

- Does this align with the work you feel called to do?
- Will this stretch you in a way that matters?
- Is this adding to the legacy you want to leave behind?

Chapter 8

That's not to say stability doesn't matter. We all have real lives and real responsibilities. Sometimes, the right next step is the one that pays the rent. But when you think with a long-game mindset, you stop making decisions out of fear or fatigue—and start moving from vision.

When I chose not to return to my agency, I wasn't rejecting stability. I was choosing alignment. I was no longer climbing just to climb. I was building.

I wanted my next move to honor my growth, my clarity, and my purpose.

That's what it means to lead beyond today.

You stop chasing a title—and start living your mission.

How I Coach for Vision

When a client comes to me at a career crossroads, they rarely start with the word vision. They usually say things like:

"I'm burned out and I don't know why."
"I feel like I'm doing everything right, yet, something's off."

"On paper, this is the job I wanted. So, why do I feel stuck?"

They're not always looking for the next step—they're looking for themselves.

And that's the heart of long-term leadership: it's not about where you're going next. It's about whether who you're becoming matches the life you're building.

That's why I never start with job titles or promotion timelines.

I start with **clarity**.

We go deep before we go forward. We name what's true before we set goals. Moving without vision isn't strategy—it's survival in disguise.

In those first sessions, I ask questions designed to bring the real story forward:

- What part of your work feels most aligned right now? What feels like a performance?
- What decisions are you making to protect your peace—and which ones are you making to protect your image?

- If you weren't worried about money or perception, what would you choose?
- What would your 5-years-from-now self thank you for?

Then, I listen—for their answers and for what their answers protect.

Vision work is delicate. It often uncovers grief—about roles they stayed in too long, opportunities they turned down, or parts of themselves they silenced to succeed. Sometimes clarity doesn't feel empowering at first—it feels sobering. But that's how you know you've found it.

You're no longer performing clarity for others.

You're telling the truth to yourself.

From there, the coaching shifts.

We start designing a life—not just a career. We sketch out possibilities. We explore aligned risks. We plan around purpose, not panic. Together, we build a roadmap that doesn't just serve their professional success—it honors their humanity.

One client recently told me, "For the first time in

my life, I'm making decisions based on who I am—not who I think I have to be."

That's vision.

That's leadership.

That's the long game.

What Clarity Feels Like

People often expect clarity to arrive like a thunderclap—a big, bold knowing that shakes everything into place.

The truth is, clarity often whispers.

It doesn't always come with certainty, but it always comes with lightness.

That's how I know I've found it—when the weight lifts. When the pressure to perform quiets down. When I stop obsessing over every single task and start aligning my energy toward something bigger.

For me, clarity feels like space.
Space to breathe.
Space to choose.
Space to stop chasing what no longer fits.

Chapter 8

It's not that everything becomes easy. But the noise quiets.

The frantic urgency settles.

The "what ifs" shrink.

And the why becomes louder than the fear.

In my coaching work, I always begin with clarity. Before goals. Before strategy. Before timelines.

If you don't know what matters to you, you'll spend your energy reacting to what matters to everyone else.

And when clarity meets insight? That's where purpose begins.

Clarity + Insight = Purpose.

That's the equation I return to again and again—for myself, and for my clients.

- **Clarity** is knowing what matters.
- **Insight** is understanding why it matters.
- **Purpose** is moving with intention toward what matters most.

That's why clarity is always the first step. It doesn't

just shift your direction—it shifts your entire relationship to the journey.

One of my clients once told me, "I didn't realize how much mental noise I'd been living with until I finally got clear. I feel lighter. Like I've finally stopped dragging things behind me."

That's what clarity feels like.

Not a blueprint—but a compass.

Not perfection—but permission.

Not a finish line—but a beginning that finally feels true.

Leadership Lesson: *Thinking Beyond Today*

There will always be another offer, another title, another opportunity that looks good on paper, yet it feels misaligned in your gut.

The higher you rise, the more tempting those offers become—because they come dressed in praise, in perks, in prestige. The real question isn't "Can I do this job?"

Chapter 8

It's "Does this job align with the leader I've become—and the legacy I want to leave?"

That's the difference between a career move and a leadership decision.

- Career moves are often reactive.
- Leadership decisions are intentional.
- Career moves respond to urgency.
- Leadership decisions respond to vision.

Thinking beyond today means resisting the impulse to leap just because the next rung is available. It means honoring your energy, your values, and your future—not just your résumé.

It means learning to sit in the discomfort of "not yet" instead of rushing into the comfort of "good enough."

The best leaders I know aren't just ambitious—they're anchored.

They don't let fear disguise itself as practicality.

They don't confuse movement with progress.

They don't chase titles—they choose alignment.

That requires deep clarity. Not about the perfect next step, but about the kind of life and leadership you're building long-term.

So, before your next decision, ask yourself:

- Does this path serve my highest vision—or just soothe my current fear?
- Am I moving because I'm growing—or because I'm uncomfortable?
- Is this opportunity an expansion—or a distraction?

The leaders who last are the ones who stop performing success and start practicing alignment.

They play the long game.

They build what they need and what others will inherit.

They lead themselves first—and they do it with intention, not urgency.

You don't need a detailed map for the next five years.

But you do need a compass.

And that compass is your vision.

Call to Action:
Craft Your 5-Year Leadership Vision

You've likely written career goals before—titles to reach, income targets to hit, promotions to chase.

But this is different.

This isn't about roles. This is about who you want to be as a leader, how you want to live, and the legacy you want to build.

Your leadership vision isn't a 5-year plan.

It's a 5-year alignment compass.

It helps you:

- Filter opportunities through purpose, not pressure
- Make decisions from clarity, not comparison
- Choose impact over image
- Stay rooted when the path isn't linear

Your Turn:
Write your 5-Year Leadership Vision Statement

Step away from the noise. Give yourself 20–30 minutes. Reflect, journal, or speak it aloud. This isn't about getting it "right"—it's about getting real.

Ask yourself:

- **How do I want to feel in my work five years from now?** *(Fulfilled? Free? Grounded? Respected?)*
- **What kind of leader do I want to be known as?** *(Collaborative? Visionary? Courageous? Healing?)*
- **Who do I want to serve—and in what way?** *(What community or cause needs your voice and leadership?)*
- **What values will I lead with—no matter the role?** *(Integrity, equity, curiosity, abundance?)*
- **What does success look like beyond salary and status?** *(Is it time freedom? Impact? Generational change? Joy?)*

Then bring it all together into 3–5 sentences.

Keep it somewhere visible. Revisit it often. Let it guide you in the moments when fear tries to disguise itself as practicality.

You don't have to have every step figured out.

But you do need a vision strong enough to follow.

Your future isn't just something you wait for.

Chapter 8

It's something you choose—one aligned decision at a time.

 Reflection

Leading from Clarity

You don't need a full plan to move forward.

But you do need clarity.

Clarity gives you direction when doubt wants to lead.

It brings peace to urgency.

It replaces overthinking with intentional action.

The truth is, you won't always feel ready. But when you are clear, you'll feel anchored—even when the path ahead is uncertain.

So, pause for a moment and ask yourself:

- What's one area of your leadership where you're seeking clarity right now?
- What story do you need to release so you can hear what your vision is really saying?
- What's one small step you can take this week—not to fix everything, but to follow your

compass?

You don't have to rush.

You don't have to prove.

You don't even have to know all the answers. You just have to choose clarity—and keep choosing it.

Clarity doesn't demand perfection.

It simply invites you to stop pretending you're lost.

You're not lost.

You're **becoming**.

> *"Clarity turns confusion into conviction. It's not about the path—it's about the permission to walk it."*
>
> —Dr. Tammi Fleming

Chapter 9
Leadership Legacy: Becoming the Leader You Needed

Opening Reflection: *What Is Legacy, Really?*

Legacy isn't your job title.

It's not your résumé, your accolades, or your LinkedIn bio.

Legacy is how people feel when they leave a room you led.

It's what lingers in the silence after you speak.

It's the shift in someone's self-belief because of something you said—or simply how you showed up.

For a long time, I thought legacy was something you earned after a long career or left behind at the end of your life. I've come to understand that legacy is built in real time—in how you live, lead, and love.

It's in the grace you extend.

The truth you tell.

The hands you hold steady behind the scenes.

The people who walk taller because of how you saw them when they felt small.

Your legacy is not what you leave for others.

It's what you leave in them.

It's not measured in grand gestures.

It's shaped in the small, consistent choices you make:

- To tell the truth when it's easier to perform
- To create space for others to rise instead of guarding your own seat
- To speak life over someone when the world has silenced them

Legacy is about impact that outlives proximity.

You don't have to be famous to have one.

You don't have to be perfect to leave one.

You just have to be present—and intentional.

At the end of the day, people won't remember the exact title you held.

They will remember how they felt in your presence.

And if they believed in themselves a little more because of you…

Chapter 9

That's legacy.

The Leaders Who Shaped Me

I've read the books, attended the conferences, sat through the trainings. Nothing has taught me more about leadership than the people who raised me, challenged me, and reflected me.

My first and greatest teacher was **Barbara Jackson**—my guardian, my anchor, and my fiercest example of leadership without a title.

Barbara didn't need a podium to be powerful. She led through sacrifice, through stillness, through consistency.

She led by organizing a rent strike, advocating for dignity, and caring for us through it all.

She wasn't interested in being impressive. She was committed to being impactful.

She wasn't the only one.

For over three decades, my husband **Felton** has been both my balance and my biggest push. We are very different—he is outgoing, effortlessly social, and moves through the world with a kind of ease that I, the introspective one, have had to learn. He'll start conversations with strangers when I'd rather observe quietly. He'll nudge me to follow up on a connection when I would've let it sit. His confidence, his grounded nature, and his ability to build relationships have stretched my leadership more than any training I've taken. We are the yin and the yang. And he has made me braver.

As I've grown into the woman, mother, and coach I am today, I now see the ripple of leadership reflected in my twin daughters.

Diamond with her sharp intellect and deep ambition, mirrors the version of me who thought excellence was the key to freedom. She's strategic, focused, and fiercely intelligent. She reminds me of the driven young leader I was; however, she leads with more ease and joy than I allowed myself.

Destiny, relational and emotionally attuned, is her father's child—and a quiet mirror of the woman I've become. She knows how to connect, how to care, how to see beneath the surface. She reminds me that

Chapter 9

leadership is also about presence, not just precision. Together, they are the best parts of me—and my greatest teachers.

Another woman who has shaped my journey in a unique and powerful way is **Regina Salliey Cooper**. Regina didn't just cheer me on—she challenged me to step out, to write this book, to stop hiding and start telling the truth. During the writing process, I called her often—sometimes in tears, sometimes laughing at my own reflections, sometimes just to hear her say, "You got this." She has been a collaborator, a witness, and a sacred sounding board. This book wouldn't exist without her encouragement and insight.

Barbara Major, another force in my life, showed me what it looks like to walk into a room and reshape it. A legend in her own right, she was president of the St. Thomas Irish Channel Consortium and is a longtime trainer with the People's Institute for Survival and Beyond. She is sharp, quick, grounded—and unapologetic. Watching her lead taught me what it means to make space where others feel powerful, not just present.

Angela Winfrey, a mentor and friend, reminds me that leadership can be joyful, even in the heavy moments. We've shared reflections, compared notes, and held space for each other as we try to do this work with purpose and with grace.

And then there was the masterclass in collaborative leadership—**Wendy Chun-Hoon, Betty Hung, and Katelyn Walker Mooney**. I had the privilege (and sometimes challenge!) of working under all three at once. Different styles, different rhythms, all brilliant. I watched and learned how leadership can look many ways—and how it can coexist beautifully when grounded in purpose and mutual respect.

Finally, **C. Mike Moreau**, the Executive Director of Kingsley House, stands out in my memory as a man who led with quiet integrity. An older white male who never assumed his experience gave him authority—he asked me, genuinely, how he could support my leadership. That humility and respect stuck with me. He didn't try to lead me. He simply created space for me to lead myself.

Chapter 9

These people didn't just influence my leadership style.

They expanded my capacity.

They helped shape the kind of coach, mother, mentor, and woman I've become.

We don't always recognize leadership in the moment.

But we feel its residue.

We carry its lessons in our bones.

And if we're lucky, we become the leader we once needed—so someone else doesn't have to walk their journey alone.

Shifting from Achievement to Impact

There was a time when every step I took was in pursuit of something that looked like success: the next title, the next salary band, the next line on the résumé that would prove I belonged in the room.

I chased achievement because I believed that achievement was the evidence of leadership.

Something shifted.

It wasn't loud. There wasn't a big moment, or a sudden breakdown. It happened slowly—over years. Through quiet realizations, in coaching sessions, in hallway conversations, in watching the eyes of someone I mentored light up when they finally saw themselves clearly.

That's when I realized:

The goal was no longer to ascend.
The goal was to expand—to multiply what I had learned in others.

I remember the first time I truly felt my influence. It wasn't in a boardroom. It wasn't on a panel. It was during a conversation with someone I had coached for months—someone who had spent their career questioning whether they were "too much" for the roles they were in.

We weren't even in session. We were walking out of a meeting, casually talking about how it went, and she paused and said:

"Because of you, I spoke up today. Even though I

Chapter 9

was scared, I remembered I didn't have to shrink to be taken seriously."

That moment hit me differently. I begin to see the ripple. I saw the reason. I saw how far I had come—from being the one who once needed permission, to being the one who could now help others give it to themselves.

That's when I started measuring my leadership differently.

Not by how many rooms I was invited into, but by how many rooms I opened up for others.

Not by the level of my title, but by the level of truth I was willing to speak.

Not by how many people followed me, but by how many people felt safe enough to find themselves in the work.

Becoming a coach made that shift even clearer.

Because coaching isn't about answers—it's about creating space. It's about listening more than directing, witnessing more than managing. Coaching required me to slow down and connect, not just drive forward. Through that, I learned that **your impact lives in the moments you're fully present—not just in the ones where you're performing**.

I used to think achievement would make me feel whole.

Now I know wholeness is what creates the kind of impact that lasts.

I no longer crave visibility for validation.

I crave resonance. I crave depth. I crave truth that travels.

When I look back at the moments that mattered most—they weren't the awards, the roles, or the impressive rooms.

They were the quiet affirmations from people who found their voice, their clarity, or their freedom in spaces we shared.

That's what I count now. That's how I lead now.

Chapter 9

Reflection

What Are You Really Building?

Take a breath. Step back from your résumé. From your calendar. From the urgent pull of the next thing.

Let's get honest.

Because achievement is easy to measure.

Impact- that's something you feel.

Use the questions below to guide your reflection:

- What have you been chasing that no longer feels fulfilling?
- How do you currently measure success—and does that definition still serve you?
- Who has been impacted by your presence, not just your performance?
- When was the last time you felt proud—not because of what you did, but because of how you showed up in the process?
- What would it look like to build something that lasts beyond applause?

You're not here to impress.

You're here to influence, to inspire, to transform.

That's impact. That's leadership. That's what lives on.

Legacy as Daily Leadership

For a long time, I thought legacy was something you earned at the end.

A final chapter. A speech at a retirement party. A name etched on a plaque.

What I've come to understand is that legacy is lived—not just left.

It's not just in the breakthroughs.
It's in the check-ins.
It's not only in the big decisions.
It's in the daily ones.

It's in how you respond when someone disappoints you.

In how you handle power when it's yours to hold—or to share.

In whether people feel seen in your presence, or

invisible behind your goals.

Legacy shows up in small, often unseen moments:

- When you pause to listen instead of pushing through an agenda
- When you create space for someone else to lead
- When you model boundaries instead of burnout
- When someone says, "Because of you, I..." and you realize they were watching—long before you noticed

One of the most humbling parts of leadership is realizing that people remember how you made them feel more than what you achieved.

That means your legacy is unfolding in real time, every coaching session, every family dinner, every team meeting.

You are building it—by how you show up.

I've had clients tell me years after a conversation that one sentence changed how they saw themselves.

I've had staff members tell me they didn't know how

to rest until they saw me take a real vacation.

I've had my children mirror back my tone, my energy, my habits—and remind me that who I am when no one is looking still matters.

That's what legacy as daily leadership means.

It's not the stage.
It's the *posture*.
It's not the spotlight.
It's the *consistency*.
It's not perfection.
It's the *practice*.

You don't need to do it all right.
You just need to do it with intention.

Because long after your title changes, people will remember how they were treated in the spaces you led.

And if you led with love, clarity, and presence—then your legacy is already in motion.

Chapter 9

Letting Go of the Need to Prove

There was a time when everything I did was quietly tied to the question:

"Am I enough?"

Even when I didn't say it out loud, it lived underneath my ambition.

It lived in the way I overprepared.

In the way I second-guessed myself even after I nailed the presentation.

In the way I made myself smaller in rooms that didn't feel built for me.

Early in my career, I led to be validated.

I led to be seen, to be heard, to be confirmed as competent, credible, worthy.

While that drive got me far, it also exhausted me.

When you lead to prove something, you never feel done. There's always one more task, one more approval, one more invisible standard to meet.

Something happens when you've done the work—the real work—of becoming and start to lead from a place of alignment, not insecurity.

You stop performing.
You stop contorting.
You stop needing to explain your value in every room.

You start leading for a different reason.

You lead to liberate.
You lead to open doors.
You lead to name truths.
You lead to create space for others to breathe.

I no longer carry the weight of proving I belong.
I know I do. Even if others don't see it—I do.
That has changed everything.

Now, I'm not chasing the next thing. I'm choosing the right thing.

I'm not managing perceptions. I'm managing my peace.
I'm not building a résumé.
I'm building a record of impact.

I show up as myself. I lead as myself. I teach others to do the same.

And that?

That's the kind of leadership I wish I'd seen more of earlier in my journey.

Now I get to model it, without apology, without performance, without the need to prove.

Just presence.
Just truth.
Just purpose.

Leadership as Inheritance: *What You're Passing On*

We don't just pass down money or assets.
We pass down stories, habits, beliefs.
We pass down ways of being in the world.

That's leadership, too.

As I reflect on my journey, I've come to realize that I'm not just building a business or a reputation—I'm building an inheritance.

Not one rooted in wealth–one rooted in wisdom.

An inheritance that my children will carry in how they lead their own lives.

That my coaching clients will carry in how they speak up, take space, and break cycles.

That my mentees will carry in the way they honor themselves while navigating systems that weren't built for them.

I used to think inheritance was about what I left behind. Now I know—it's also about what I leave within.

Here's what I'm passing on:

- The belief that your story matters—even the messy parts
- The strength to say no to good things in pursuit of right things
- The reminder that leadership is not a performance—it's a responsibility
- The courage to ask for help without shame
- The freedom to walk away from spaces that require you to shrink

Above all, I want to pass on this truth:
You do not have to become someone else to lead powerfully.

Chapter 9

You already have what you need inside of you.

What I've learned, unlearned, and healed—I pass on.

Not because I have it all figured out. Because I now understand that impact is inherited.

Every healed part of me is a door opened for someone else.

I hope those who come after me don't have to fight the same battles to feel seen, to lead boldly, or to live in alignment.

I hope they start further ahead because I stood where I did.

A Letter To the Ones Coming Behind Me

Dear Future Leader,

I wrote this for you.
Not because I have all the answers, but because I know what it feels like to have the questions- and not have anyone to ask (for answers).
I know what it's like to walk into rooms where your brilliance is questioned before you speak. To feel the weight of proving you belong—when you've already earned your seat.
To quiet your voice just to survive the moment,
while something inside you longs to lead differently.
I've been there.
And if there's one thing I want you to know, it's this:
You are not too much.
You are not too late.
You are not too different.
You are being shaped—on purpose—for impact.
You don't need to become anyone else to lead powerfully.
You don't need another title to be taken seriously.
You don't have to wait until it's perfect, until you feel

Chapter 9

ready, until someone else says yes.

Start now.

Lead from where you are. Trust that your presence is already doing the work.

Lead with clarity.

Lead with care.

Lead with your whole self.

When you feel unsure, tired, or unseen—remember:

You are part of a legacy that is still unfolding.

You are not alone. You are the next chapter of someone else's breakthrough.

Keep going. You are the leader we've been waiting for.

With love and conviction,

Dr. Tammi Fleming

> "When I dare to be powerful—to use my strength in the service of my vision—then it becomes less and less important whether I am afraid."
> —Audre Lorde

Acknowledgments

Writing this book has been one of the most vulnerable, courageous, and clarifying things I've ever done. And I didn't do it alone. I couldn't have.

To my husband, **Felton**, the powerful force behind every success I've ever had. Your love, bold support, and steady belief in me have given me the strength to rise. Though you may not be visible in my professional world, your presence is felt in every step I take. You never asked me to be less–only how far I could go. This is our victory too.

To my children—**Alisa, Felton Jr., Kanecha, Fernail, Tyriek, Feltonisha, Diamond, Damara,** and **Destiny**— you are the greatest leadership experience of my life. Watching each of you grow, graduate, and lead in your own way has been my deepest joy. You are my why.

To **Duchess**, my four-legged shadow and source of calm —thank you for keeping me grounded—and making even the hardest writing days a little softer.

To **Bill Buckner**, my mentor, thought partner, and friend—thank you for continuing to challenge me to think bigger, deeper, and with more clarity. Your belief in me has helped me believe in myself.

To **Marian Urquilla**, my executive coach and calm in the storm. Your questions unraveled everything I thought I knew—and helped me rebuild from a place of truth. You guided me out of reaction and into reflection. I carry your insight in every room I enter.

To **Regina Salliey Cooper**, who talked me off the ledge when I needed it most. You held me through a time when everything felt uncertain. Your words—"Girl, you can do this. You are brilliant. You will survive"—played on repeat in my heart. Thank you for seeing me when I couldn't fully see myself.

To **Dr. Janice Johnson Dias**—thank you for the tremendous honor of writing the foreword to this book. I am still ecstatic you said yes. Your brilliance, bold leadership, and unwavering commitment to truth inspire me deeply. Your words set the tone for this journey, and your legacy reminds us all what it means to lead with purpose and power.

To **Donna Knuckles**, my book and writing coach—thank you for helping me develop a coherent strategy and for reminding me to give myself the time to produce work that reflects my truth and excellence. Your thoughtful edits, feedback, and encouragement made me a better writer and helped me speak more directly to my audience.

To **Diamond**, the creative force behind the book's social media campaign—thank you for giving this work a digital heartbeat. Your eye for design, strategy, and storytelling continues to amplify the message and expand its reach.

To **Barbara Major** and **Katrina Trumble**, my alpha readers—thank you for your honesty, time, and commitment to helping me preserve an authentic voice. Your insights were invaluable.

To the **leaders**, **colleagues**, and **communities** I've served over the years—thank you for the trust, the tension, the breakthroughs, and the detours. You have shaped me.

To **every Black woman** who has ever felt unseen in leadership spaces—this book is a mirror and a message. You belong. You've always belonged. Let your brilliance take up space.

To my birth mother, **Josephine**—I know how deeply you loved us, even through your struggles. In another world, you would have been a leader too. Thank you for your pride in me and the spirit you passed on.

And finally, to **you**, the reader—thank you for letting me be part of your journey. If these words help you see yourself more clearly, or lead more boldly, then it was all worth it.

With deep gratitude and unwavering hope,

Tammi Fleming

Glossary of Key Terms

Adaptive Leadership
A leadership framework that emphasizes navigating change, managing uncertainty, and helping people adapt by facing difficult realities and shifting behaviors.

Coaching (Executive or Leadership)
A structured, confidential partnership focused on personal and professional growth. It helps leaders build self-awareness, enhance performance, and reach their goals through deep inquiry, reflection, and accountability.

Emotional Intelligence (EQ)
The ability to recognize, understand, and manage your own emotions—and to navigate and influence the emotions of others. Core elements include self-awareness, self-regulation, motivation, empathy, and relationship management.

Executive Presence
A blend of voice, visibility, and vibe. It's how others experience you in high-stakes moments—your confidence, clarity, calm, and ability to inspire trust and credibility.

Leadership Plateau

A stage in a leader's career where growth feels stalled despite continued effort. Often a signal that technical expertise must give way to adaptive skills and new strategies for influence.

360 Feedback

A leadership development tool that gathers feedback from multiple levels—supervisors, peers, direct reports, and sometimes external partners—to provide a full view of performance, behaviors, and perception.

Resources & References

The Practice of Adaptive Leadership journey is lifelong. If this book sparked something in you, here are some of the key tools, frameworks, and readings that supported my growth and may enrich yours as well.

Books Referenced or Inspired By:
- Goleman, Daniel. Emotional Intelligence: Why It Can Matter More Than IQ.
- Heifetz, Ronald & Linsky, Marty. Leadership on the Line: Staying Alive Through the Dangers of Leading.
- Stone, Douglas; Patton, Bruce; & Heen, Sheila. Difficult Conversations: How to Discuss What Matters Most.
- Brown, Brené. Dare to Lead: Brave Work. Tough Conversations. Whole Hearts.

Research & Tools:
- International Coaching Federation (ICF), Global Coaching Client Study – showing 70% of coachees report improved performance, communication, and relationships.
- EQ-i 2.0® – Emotional intelligence assessment and development model.

- 360° Leadership Feedback – A process of collecting anonymous feedback from direct reports, peers, and supervisors.
- Adaptive Leadership Framework – Developed by Ronald Heifetz at Harvard Kennedy School.
- American Psychological Association. (n.d.). Impostor syndrome. In APA Dictionary of Psychology. Retrieved from https://dictionary.apa.org/impostor-syndrome

About the Author

Dr. Tammi Fleming is an executive coach, strategist, and speaker who helps mission-driven professionals step into leadership with clarity, confidence, and purpose. With more than three decades of experience across the nonprofit, philanthropic, and public sectors—including a presidential appointment as a federal equity fellow—she brings both insight and heart to her work.

Tammi holds a Ph.D. in Public Health and is a certified executive coach, yet she believes her greatest credential is her ability to listen deeply and challenge gently. She lives in Pennsylvania with her husband, their beloved Shih Tzu Duchess, and their three of their young adult children who keep her grounded and inspired.

To learn more, visit:
diamondconsultantsllc.com
Connect with Tammi on:
LinkedIn: linkedin.com/in/tammifleming0918
Facebook: facebook.com/tammi.fleming.1

A Note on the Interior Design & Visual Storytelling

The look and feel of The Leadership Detour—from the content flow to the layout of the companion guide—reflects the intentional design of **Euferose Correa White**. With a Master's in Education and deep expertise in learner-centered design, she brought clarity, accessibility, and elegance to each page. Her work bridges knowledge and visual storytelling with purpose and beauty.

To connect or collaborate, email elearnwitheuferose@gmail.com or visit: elearnwitheuferose.my.canva.site/id-portfolio

Destiny White, the visual storyteller behind this project, brought it to life with creativity and precision. From hand-drawing every icon and prompt to translating abstract ideas into compelling visuals, her fingerprints are on every element. With a background in media production and a gift for design, Destiny animated the book campaign, illustrated the companion guide, and reimagined the companion cover to mirror the heart of the original. Her vision and craft shaped the emotional and visual language of this work.

To explore or collaborate, email destinytwhite7@gmail.com, or visit: destinytwhite7.wixsite.com/destiny-white